Essays in
Scotch-Irish Hist

Essays in
Scotch-Irish History

edited by

E.R.R. GREEN

with a new Introduction by

Steve Ickringill

ULSTER HISTORICAL FOUNDATION

List of Contributors

The Late Professor E. R. R. Green was Director of the Institute of Irish Studies
at the Queen's University of Belfast.

Arthur S. Link is George Henry Davis Professor of American History,
Emeritus, Princeton University.

Esmond Wright is Director of the Institute of United States Studies,
Emeritus, University of London.

Maldwyn A. Jones is Commonwealth Fund Professor of American History,
Emeritus, University of London.

The Late Professor E. Estyn Evans was Director of the Institute of Irish Studies
at the Queen's University of Belfast.

First published 1969
by Routledge & Kegan Paul Ltd

© *E. R. R. Green* 1969

This edition published 1992 *by*
The Ulster Historical Foundation
12 *College Square East, Belfast, BT*1 6*DD*

ISBN 0 901905 53 4

Printed by W. & G. Baird Ltd, Antrim

The Ulster Historical Foundation's Publications Programme receives
financial assistance under the Cultural Traditions Programme which
aims to encourage acceptance and understanding of Cultural diversity.

Cover design by Wendy Dunbar

Foreword

By His Grace The Duke of Abercorn, H.M.L.,
President of the Ulster-Scot Historical Foundation

This volume of essays in Scotch-Irish history is the second volume
in the Society's Historical Series. The papers were originally
delivered as lectures at a Symposium sponsored by the Foundation
and held at the Queen's University, Belfast, in September 1965.
These lectures aroused considerable interest and as they also repre-
sent important contributions to original research it has been
thought desirable that they should be given permanent form by
publication in this Series. The Foundation is indebted to the distinguished scholars who delivered the lectures in Belfast and prepared
them for publication, and to Dr E. R. R. Green who undertook
the responsibilities of editorship. In addition I should like to thank
the Vice-Chancellor of the Queen's University of Belfast, the
Consul-General of the United States of America in Belfast and
the Government of Northern Ireland, all of whom helped in the
success of the Symposium by providing both accommodation and
hospitality to those attending.

When the Foundation was established in 1957 (it was called the
Ulster-Scot Historical Society until March 1969) to foster interest
in the history of the Ulster-Scots, publication was regarded as a
main aim. Dr Dickson's volume on Ulster emigration to colonial
America in the eighteenth century has had an encouraging reception and I hope that this volume dealing more directly with the
Ulster-Scot in North America will be equally well received.

Illustrations

Contents

Introduction

The re-publication of this collection of essays is a great tribute to the scholars involved in its original production, and to the project's inspiration, Professor E. R. R. Green, in particular. Although some of my concentration in what follows is a brief discussion of work in 'Scotch-Irish' history published in the last twenty years or so, a re-reading of these essays emphasises their continuing worth and demands a response in this new introduction. Just as Leyburn's work a generation or so before the original publication of these essays clearly inspired the contributors to this collection, so their work has continued to encourage other scholars. Indeed, perhaps most notably in the case of Professor M. A. Jones, the contributors themselves have further developed their topic—a topic which has often and will often inspire controversy. The very term 'Scotch-Irish' is always likely to see some hackles rise, and no-one could accuse these essays of blandness, or make such a charge of the best of the work that has followed since their first publication.

For someone who has taught United States history survey courses for many years, Professor Link's essay is intriguing. I, like thousands of others, have used his exhaustive works on the whole of Woodrow Wilson's career. I think it fair to say that in these volumes Link has little or nothing to say about Wilson's Scotch-Irish heritage. He does, of course, have much to say about his Presbyterian background, and indeed the Presbyterianism which was at the foreground of Wilson's life. This is, of course, at the heart of what Link himself says in his essay. It is a point of central importance. For most, if not all, writers, the history of the Presbyterian Church in the American colonies and then in the United States is fused with the narrative of the Scotch-Irish people (or 'race', as the enthusiasts of the Scotch-Irish Congresses of the late nineteenth century would have said). Professor Wright is a particularly vigorous example of such a commentator. Woodrow Wilson as an individual was something of an Anglophile, who knew and seemed to care more about England

Introduction

than he did about Scotland or Ireland. Yet, as a man imbued with Calvinism he was willy-nilly involved in the Scotch-Irish, Scottish and New England experience. It is certainly true that Wilson eschewed involvement with the Scotch-Irish Societies of the late nineteenth century. Unlike some of his professional colleagues at Princeton such as Professors Frederick Willson and George McCloskie, his name is not found among the office holders of the national Scotch-Irish Society or its local branches. Woodrow Wilson was not even a member.

To try and understand Wilson's absence of involvement, it is helpful to discuss some prominent political figures in order to fill out Professor Link's portrait of one individual with references to others. William McKinley and Adlai Stevenson (the first!) were just two such examples. McKinley, though self-consciously aware of his background, was always determined to emphasise tolerance of other groups and their massive contributions to the United States. My impression is that Stevenson was similarly perhaps a little uneasy about some of the more virulent claims made by late nineteenth-century Scotch-Irish enthusiasts. Speaking as Governor of Ohio, McKinley was keen to emphasise the worth of all (or nearly all)—'Here the Puritan and Cavalier, the Protestant and Catholic, the Englishman and Irishman, the German and Frenchman, the Scotch-Irish and the Pure Celt, live together in harmony and fraternity as American citizens . . .' For all this very proper magnanimity, McKinley in front of his 'own' (a term also used by Governor Hastings of Pennsylvania on a similar occasion) could let his hair down and announce:

> the Americanized Scotch-Irishman is the perfection of a type which is the development of the commingling and assimilating procedures of centuries. Before he loses his racial distinctiveness and individuality he should be photographed by history's camera, although for long years to come his identity will manifest itself in the composite presentment of the future typical American.

James G. Blaine and McKinley's own *eminence grise* Marcus Hanna also had a Scotch-Irish background. I hope the point with relevance to Woodrow Wilson is now clear. Wilson was a Democrat and a singularly large number of prominent Republicans were more or less self-consciously Scotch-Irish. Despite his name,

Introduction

Theodore Roosevelt was keen to emphasise his Scotch-Irish blood-lines, and if one were to note Governors of *the* Scotch-Irish state, Pennsylvania, the list would become tediously long. This reality of American party political history is nicely, if a little curiously, emphasised by Dennis Clark (*The Irish in Philadelphia*, Philadelphia, 1973) when he observes the political realities facing Irish *Catholics* in the city:

> It confirmed the Irish Catholics either to political futility in the ranks of an ineffectual Democratic Party or to the status of permanent minority stepchildren within the ranks of a republican organization dominated locally by Anglo-Saxon businessmen and statewide by *Scotch-Irish* [my emphasis] political bosses?

Although for solid political reasons it was unlikely that Woodrow Wilson would make much of his Scotch-Irishness, others, Republicans, could and did.

This emphasis so far in my introduction on the late nineteenth century, and an attempt to approach Link's contribution from another angle, may be unexpected, but it is quite deliberate. The obvious thing about this collection of work and of most of what has been written on the Scotch-Irish is its relatively early chrono-logical focus. There is a kind of understanding, perhaps agree-ment, among historians and historical geographers. Put crudely, the eighteenth century was the Scotch-Irish period, the nineteenth and twentieth centuries the years when the sensible focus is on Irish Catholics and their contribution to the United States. This is seen to reflect the realities of patterns of immigration from Ireland to North America. I am not daring to challenge this orthodoxy in any fundamental way, but perhaps a modest caveat might be allowed. Marjorie R. Fallows (*Irish Americans: Identity and Assimilations*, Englewood Cliffs, 1979) observes that however difficult and controversial the methodology, it can be argued that, using information gleaned from the 1970 U.S. Census, as many as 50% of those identifying as themselves as 'Irish' in terms of their ancestral background were Protestant. Fallows, basing her discus-sion on the work of other scholars, notably Andrew M. Greeley (*Ethnicity in the United States: A Preliminary Reconnaissance*, New York, 1974), notes that Scotch-Irish was not a category offered to people for a description of their own sense of their origins. She assumes that overwhelmingly these 'Protestant-Irish' were

Introduction

descendants of the great Scotch-Irish settlement of the colonial, revolutionary and early national periods. Even if she is right we are still talking about between one and two million people who must have had a more recent immigrant background. On a more trivial note in terms of statistics, I calculate that nearly 25% of the national membership of the Scotch-Irish Society of Americans in 1895 were born in Ireland (nearly all in Ulster), and that of the membership in California 80% were Irish born!

This does lead us into a concluding discussion on the main thrust of these essays in Scotch-Irish history. I am suggesting an underestimation of the importance and size of the Scotch-Irish community (if the word is appropriate) in nineteenth- and twentieth-century America. In a way rather similarly some scholars have urged us to think again about the balance between Protestant and Catholic immigrants in the eighteenth century. David N. Doyle (*Ireland, Irishmen and Revolutionary America*, Cork, 1981) has perhaps developed the case most effectively for understanding the numbers of those with a Catholic Irish background by the time of the American Revolution. Interestingly, *the* essential book on emigration to North America from Ulster in the eighteenth century remains the same now as it was in 1969. R. J. Dickson (*Ulster Emigration to Colonial America*, Belfast, 1966, and with a new introduction by G. E. Kirkham, 1988) remains a remarkably durable standard. Indeed, as I indicated at the outset of this introduction, some names in addition to Dickson remain very relevant, and chief among them is Professor M. A. Jones.

The most useful thing anyone interested in following up what Wright, Jones, Evans and Green had to say is to read M. A. Jones ('The Scotch Irish in British America' in B. Bailyn and P. D. Morgans eds, *Strangers within the Realm*, Chapel Hill, 1991, pp. 284–313) with particular attention to his exemplary footnotes. I propose to pick out a few examples of work that seems obviously tied to the concerns of our essayists, while allowing myself one brief, perhaps pertinent, aside. W. R. Brock (*Scotus Americanus: A Survey of the Sources for Links between Scotland and America in the Eighteenth Century*, Edinburgh, 1982) described the Scottish Highlanders in colonial times as 'the shock troops' thrown at the frontier. Those who have worked on the Scotch-Irish would probably wish to get involved in a squabble here, for what were the Irish Presbyterians but 'the shock troops' thrown at frontier

Introduction

after frontier? It is too easy to become involved in comparable squabbles and all are variously guilty, including extreme examples from Michael J. O'Brien ('The Scotch Irish Myth', *Journal of the American Irish Historical Society*, 1925, 142–153) to Grady McWhinney (*Cracker Culture: Celtic Ways in the Old South*, Tuscaloosa, 1988).

There certainly is a great disagreement over whether the Scotch-Irish were really distinctive or just part of a wider and underestimated 'Celtic' component of colonial and early national America. The starting point is to read E. S. and F. McDonald ('The Ethnic Origins of the American People, 1790', *William and Mary Quarterly*, XXXVII 1980, pp. 179–199). It seems fair to suggest that those interested in Scottish, Irish, Welsh, English, particularly Cornish-English, history are unlikely to be persuaded by the all-embracing Celtic label. Similarly, close analysis of certain areas of crisis in revolutionary America would lead to many doubts. O. S. Ireland ('The Ethnic-Religious Dimension of Pennsylvania Politics, 1778–1779', *William and Mary Quarterly*, XXX (1973), pp. 423–449) has argued effectively for exactly what his title implies for the Scotch-Irish and their 'Calvinist' allies. Calvinism, Presbyterianism and the Scotch-Irish remains one of the most discussed and central themes. In my view, the most central and important work published recently is M. J. Westerkamp (*Triumph of the Laity: Scots-Irish Piety and the Great Awakening*, New York, 1988). Here the complicated and intriguing interplay of theology, church organisation and ethnicity is teased out. What was distinctively Scottish as against Scotch-Irish in the evolving Presbyterian tradition is discussed. Perhaps most memorably, the Ulster background to American 'Revivalism' is emphasised. To return to my own favourite concern, it is clear that those who were most self-consciously 'Scotch-Irish' five generations after the American Revolution were usually, equally, self-consciously Presbyterian. Indeed, like many of their predecessors, they were likely to be involved in some ongoing theological and organisational debate within the Presbyterian tradition as they saw it.

Clearly it would be possible and, in an ideal world, proper to list the work of many more scholars. Whatever else it would be fatuous to ignore the work of K. A. Miller (*Emigrants and Exiles: Ireland and the Irish Exodus to North America*, Oxford, 1985). It seems particularly apposite to note Miller's major contribution, as he insists

Introduction

that as much as 70% of the Protestant emigrants to Colonial British America were Presbyterians. Having noted Miller's work, why not R. S. Wallace, J. F. Hart, T. Parkhill, T. Blethen, C. Wood, M. Bric, and many others? If one considers the specialist scholars of Ireland and Scotland who could be added, the inadequacy of this survey would be even more obvious. What is equally obvious is that, as all of those interested in the past like to say, much more work remains to be done. Perhaps a little unexpectedly, once more, that determined historian of Irish *Catholics* in Philadelphia, Dennis Clark, makes part of the point in a footnote:

> It would add greatly to the coherence of the history of the Irish in the United States if the fortunes of both Protestant and Catholic Irishmen could be treated as a whole. But because of differences between the two groups in cycles of emigration, cultural and religious traditions, and social position, such a united treatment would be a false reconciliation that would contradict the reality of the antipathy that has so disastrously divided the groups since the seventeenth century.

Perhaps a little perversely this view ensures that essays in Scotch-Irish history will continue to be written because, for some at least, the great divide is just that. It can only be hoped that future essays achieve the standards of calmness and balance manifest in this now re-published collection. However, the sneaking hope remains that one future such essay might be devoted to the discussion of how it was that that most impeccably Scotch-Irish of American Presidents, Andrew Jackson, (conceived, it is thought, in Carrickfergus, born in North America), could appeal vigorously and confidently to the Irish vote devoid of any suggestion of sectarian differences. Others interested in this topic may well be persuaded into scholarship on other relevant themes by reading the essays that follow this brief introduction.

S. J. S. Ickringill,
University of Ulster

Editor's Introduction

It was in North America that the term Scotch-Irish originated. No such hyphenation existed in Ireland, where differences of nationality merged all too easily into differences of religion. Yet to begin with it was an accurate enough description of Presbyterian immigrants from Ireland whose recent forbears had come from Scotland. Nor was the name always used in a complimentary sense. An Irish parson, sent by the Society for the Propagation of the Gospel to South Carolina, complained in 1711 that an English clergyman there had called him a 'Scotch-Irish Lyllibolaro'.[1] This was to accuse him of being a Presbyterian and a Whig, for Lillibolaro was the song which had been on the lips of every opponent of James II in 1688. To jeer at the Ulsterman's mixed nationality was an obvious taunt. The Irish and the Germans were, after all, the new immigrants of the eighteenth century, and were bound to come in for some abuse from those who had been there a generation or two longer.

The Scots who had settled in Ulster only began to remigrate to the North American colonies towards the end of the seventeenth century, and the real tide of emigration did not set in until after 1715. Ulster then became one of the most important sources of addition to the population for something like a century. There has accordingly been a tendency to associate the Scotch-Irish with the Colonial period of American history. It is understandable why this should be so, for although Ulstermen no doubt emigrated in even greater numbers in the nineteenth century, relatively they formed a much smaller group in the population. This was also the heroic period of Scotch-Irish history whose glory has not been entirely dimmed by the well sustained attacks of more recent historians on their reputation as frontiersmen *par excellence*, as planters of church organisation and education in the wilderness, and as valiant upholders of the cause of American independence.

In the history of Ulster emigration, the American Revolution

[1] Frank J. Klingberg (ed.), 'Carolina Chronicle, the Papers of Commissary Gideon Johnston, 1707–1716', *University of California Publications in History*, Vol. XXXV (1946), p. 84.

was only a temporary interruption and the tide flowed as strongly after 1783 as before. But there was a difference in attitude among many emigrants. In the glow of optimism and fraternity shed by the rising sun of European revolution, old divisions were forgotten and the simple name of Irishman became a sufficient identity. This did not last, but on the other hand the greater mobility and wider opportunity of life in nineteenth-century America meant that there were to be no more compact Scotch-Irish settlements such as there had been in the past. The Ulster immigrant now found his place as an individual in the United States, and in a society which placed fewer obstacles in the way of his absorption than of most foreigners.

The Scotch-Irish tradition persisted nonetheless and emerged with renewed self-consciousness in the later years of the century. This can no doubt be explained in terms of a reaction against the mass immigration from Southern Ireland which followed the Great Famine of 1846–7 and with which the older stock had no desire to be associated. Yet there were other factors such as the existence of the Presbyterian Church as an American institution but to a large extent Irish in origin. The desire to bind up the wounds inflicted by the Civil War was also evident, especially in the annual Scotch-Irish congresses which met for over a decade at the end of the century. Yet the individuals who organised these gatherings had little more in common with the immigrants of a century before than the right to call themselves Scotch-Irish. No longer an intrusive group, they were now Americans so confident of their identity that they could celebrate their Scots and Irish lineage. The purpose of their association naturally determined the nature of much of the historical writing which emerged and was also responsible for the defects of which present-day historians strongly complain.

The Ulster-Scot Historical Foundation hopes to do somewhat better while fully realising the difficulties and pitfalls which beset those who venture into immigrant studies. A few of these might with advantage be mentioned at this point. To begin with, it is necessary not only to possess a detailed knowledge of the history of more than one country, but the ability to approach differing and often conflicting cultures with sympathy and understanding. Immigrant groups too, are by their nature doomed to eventual extinction and it is never easy to determine at what point assimilation is complete and the study became genealogical rather than social. On a more mundane level, the field involves expensive travel in pursuit of widely scattered sources of information, if the job is to be well done.

As a first approach, it was decided to invite a number of scholars to contribute to a lecture series with the aim of establishing the outlines of Scotch-Irish history as a field of inquiry and also to stimulate further research with consistent aims and methods. In the first essay, Professor Link has considered the possible effect on a great American president of his Scotch-Irish inheritance, and seen the connection in the vitality of his Presbyterian faith. Professor Wright draws attention to the fact that the Scotch-Irish experience involved Scotland as well as Ulster and North America and explores the educational links between the three areas. The most conventional and at the same time the most original contribution is from Professor Jones, who subjects the neglected transitional period of the history of emigration from Ulster between 1783 and 1815 to close and careful scrutiny. Professor Evans, drawing on his deep knowledge of Irish rural life, makes a plea for an interdisciplinary approach in determining the possible influence of the Scotch-Irish on patterns of settlement, land and the nature of society in the Old West. The editorial contribution is by way of a test of the use to which a special type of source material, emigrant correspondence, can be put by the historian. It is to be hoped that the essays will achieve their aim in inaugurating a new period of activity in the writing of Scotch-Irish history, a term which might well be retained to cover exploration of the many and fascinating links between Ulster and the United States.

CHAPTER I

Woodrow Wilson and His Presbyterian Inheritance

by Arthur S. Link

I: THE FAMILY AND RELIGIOUS INHERITANCE OF WOODROW WILSON

I would like to say how happy I am to participate in this significant conference. Perhaps at some future time it may be regarded as historic because it marked the beginning of an organised, formal concern for the long and fruitful Scotch-Irish-American connection. This tiny island of Ireland has made, during the past three centuries, a greater contribution to the character and development of the American people than any other territory of comparable size and population on the face of the earth.

Permit me also to say a brief word about what I hope to do in this lecture. I have not come across the water to talk generally and sentimentally about the Scotch-Irish-American connection, for I have neither the ability nor the disposition for such an effort. I had originally planned to focus on Woodrow Wilson's Scotch-Irish inheritance. But one very poor draft of a lecture along these lines persuaded me that it is impossible to deal in any separate manner with Woodrow Wilson's Scotch-Irish inheritance. When one begins to talk about Wilson's Scotch-Irish inheritance one runs squarely into the fact that Wilson had an equally important, if not more important, Scottish inheritance, and that it is literally impossible to separate the two strands in his biography.

What, I asked myself, as I thrashed about trying to make a new start, was the one aspect of Wilson's inheritance that stemmed both from Scotland and Northern Ireland and was unique? In other words, why was Wilson different because he was of Scotch-Irish and Scottish descent? The answer is not long in coming to anyone familiar with Woodrow Wilson. He was different from a descendant of German or Anglican English immigrants because he was a Calvinist and a Presbyterian. Every biographer of Woodrow Wilson has said that it is impossible to know and understand the man apart from his religious faith, because his every action and policy was ultimately informed and moulded by his Christian faith. This is true, but it is even more important to say that Woodrow Wilson was a Presbyterian Christian of the Calvinistic persuasion. He stands pre-eminent among all the inheritors of that tradition who have made significant contributions to American political history. Indeed, he was the prime embodiment, the apogee, of the Calvinistic tradition among all statesmen of the modern epoch.

Woodrow Wilson, thirteenth President of Princeton University, forty-third Governor of New Jersey, and twenty-eighth President of the United States, was of undiluted Scottish and Scotch-Irish descent, and the sheer weight of historical evidence tempts one to say that he was predestined to be a Presbyterian. His ancestors in Scotland and Ireland had been Presbyterians since the Reformation. His mother, Janet Woodrow, was born in Carlisle, England, on 20 December 1830. Her father, the Reverend Thomas Woodrow, was a Scottish Presbyterian minister who migrated with his family from Carlisle to the New World in 1835–6 and, after a brief and cold sojourn in Canada in 1836–7, settled in Ohio and held pulpits in that state and in Kentucky. Thomas Woodrow in turn was descended from Patrick Woodrow, a Roman Catholic priest who became a Presbyterian minister and married at the time of the Scottish Reformation. His descendants down to Thomas Woodrow were prominent Presbyterian ministers and elders. One of Thomas Woodrow's sons, the Reverend Doctor James Woodrow, was long a professor at the Presbyterian Theological Seminary in Columbia, South Carolina, and the publisher of two of the leading American Presbyterian journals in the late nineteenth century, *The Southern Presbyterian*, a weekly newspaper, and *The Southern Presbyterian Review*, a quarterly.[1]

---

[1] Marion W. Woodrow (ed.), *Dr James Woodrow As Seen by His Friends* (Columbia, S.C., 1909), *passim*.

Woodrow Wilson and His Presbyterian Inheritance

Woodrow Wilson's father was the Reverend Doctor Joseph Ruggles Wilson, born at Steubenville, Ohio, on 28 February 1822. He married Janet Woodrow on 7 June 1849, and, after holding a pastorate in Pennsylvania, settled in Virginia, where he was a professor at Hampden-Sidney College from 1851 to 1855 and then pastor of the First Presbyterian Church in Staunton from 1855 to 1857. Joseph Ruggles Wilson was afterwards pastor in Augusta, Georgia, a professor at the Columbia Theological Seminary, pastor in Wilmington, North Carolina, and professor at the Southwestern Presbyterian University in Clarksville, Tennessee.

Joseph Ruggles Wilson was in turn the son of James Wilson, who was born near Londonderry on 20 February 1787, and migrated to Philadelphia in 1807. There are Wilsons who bear a striking physical resemblance to Joseph Ruggles Wilson and Woodrow Wilson still living in the Wilson homestead at Dergalt near Londonderry. This cottage is almost certainly the one in which James Wilson was born, although historical research has failed to establish incontrovertible evidence that this is so,[1] or, for that matter, evidence about the parents of James Wilson.

A printer who learned his trade in Gray's Printing Shop in Strabane, James Wilson worked on the Philadelphia *Aurora*, a Jeffersonian newspaper, from 1807 to 1815. He married a Scotch-Irish lass, Ann Adams, whom he met on the boat to America, in the Fourth Presbyterian Church in Philadelphia on 1 November 1808, and seven sons and three daughters were born to this union. The Wilsons moved to Steubenville, Ohio, in 1815, so that James Wilson could assume the editorship of the *Western Herald and Steubenville Gazette*. He was active in business and in Ohio politics, serving several times in the General Assembly and as associate judge of the Court of Common Pleas. He died of cholera on 17 October 1850.[2]

Woodrow Wilson was born in the Presbyterian manse in Staunton, Virginia, on 28 or 29 December 1856, and grew up in manses in Augusta, Columbia, and Wilmington. Thus he had, as

---

[1] Kenneth Darwin to the author, 11 Nov. 1965. Both the Wilson cottage and Gray's Printing Shop are now National Trust properties, the Wilson family having removed to a residence nearby. For descriptions of both these properties, see *Wilson House* and *Gray's Printing Press* (National Trust, 1967).

[2] Francis P. Weisenburger, 'The Middle Western Antecedents of Woodrow Wilson', *Mississippi Valley Historical Review*, XXIII (Dec. 1936), pp. 375–90; Edwin M. Stark to the author, 3 May 1966.

he once put it, 'the unspeakable joy of having been born and bred in a minister's family'. It was a family bound together by strong ties of love and dominated by a strong-willed father who valued education along with Christian faith. Young Woodrow grew up on family worship, Bible reading, study of the *Shorter Catechism*, and stories of Scottish Covenanters. As he later said in a speech in London on his sixty-second birthday, 'The stern Covenanter tradition that is behind me sends many an echo down the years.' Admitted to the membership of the First Presbyterian Church of Columbia on 5 July 1873, he also grew up in the bosom of the church, imbibing unconsciously its traditions and faith. Woodrow Wilson's father, Joseph Ruggles Wilson, was not only a distinguished minister but also one of the founders of the Presbyterian Church in the Confederate States of America, re-named the Presbyterian Church in the United States in 1865, and commonly called the southern Presbyterian Church. Doctor Wilson was Moderator of the General Assembly of that denomination in 1879 and Permanent Clerk and Stated Clerk of the General Assembly from 1861 to 1898. It is possible that Woodrow Wilson attended the meetings in his father's church in Augusta in April 1861 when the decision was taken to form the southern Presbyterian Church. In any event, he later became his father's right-hand man in correspondence relating to church business and in preparing the minutes of the General Assembly for publication. Doctor Wilson also edited the Wilmington *North Carolina Presbyterian* in 1876–7, and young Woodrow not only helped to edit the paper but also contributed a series of articles in 1876—the first that he ever published.[1] Church leaders were constantly in the Wilson home, and church affairs was a major subject of family correspondence and discussion.

Woodrow Wilson was inordinately proud of his family inheritance and especially of the fact that he, rather strikingly, re-united in his own person the Scottish and Scotch-Irish stock. He knew his grandfather Thomas Woodrow very well and visited Carlisle several times in efforts to find the manse in which his mother had been born and the church in which his grandfather had preached. He of course never saw his grandfather Wilson. Woodrow Wilson constantly referred in speeches and conversations to his ancestry

[1] They are printed in Arthur S. Link *et al.* (eds.), *The Papers of Woodrow Wilson* (Princeton, N.J., 1967), Vol. I.

and often remarked playfully about its manifestations in his own personality. To his Scottish ancestors he attributed his introspection, seriousness, and tendency toward melancholy. To his Irish forbears he attributed his occasional gaiety and love of life. Once, half joking, half serious, he told his students at Bryn Mawr College, 'No one who amounts to anything is without some Scotch-Irish blood.'

II: WOODROW WILSON, PRESBYTERIAN

Woodrow Wilson's inheritance, both from Scotland and Northern Ireland, and from his own immediate family on the Wilson and Woodrow sides, laid strong foundations for Christian faith in mature life. '*My* life', he told a friend when he was President of the United States, 'would not be worth living if it were not for the driving power of religion, for *faith*, pure and simple. I have seen all my life the arguments against it without ever having been moved by them. . . . There are people who *believe* only so far as they *understand*—that seems to me presumptuous and sets their understanding as the standard of the universe.'[1] Wilson was apparently never buffeted by strong winds, much less storms, of doubt. His adult faith found expression, among other ways, in family worship, daily prayer, Bible reading—it has been said that he wore out several Bibles reading them—and, above all, active church membership. He and his family were members, successively, of the Bryn Mawr, Pennsylvania, Presbyterian Church, the Congregational Church of Middletown, Connecticut, the Second Presbyterian Church of Princeton, and the First Presbyterian Church of that same town. He was ordained a Ruling Elder in 1897 and served on the sessions of both Princeton churches.

Wilson and his wife resumed their relationship with the southern Presbyterian denomination in which they had both been reared by moving their membership to the Central Presbyterian Church when they went to Washington in 1913. It was a small congregation, and Wilson loved its simple service—it took him back, he said, to the days when he was a boy in the South. He attended as regularly as possible until 1919, when illness confined him to his home, and he showed his concern in ways large and small. He also developed a warm friendship with the church's pastor,

[1] Arthur S. Link, *Wilson: The New Freedom* (Princeton, N.J., 1956), pp. 64-5.

Doctor James H. Taylor, that lasted until Wilson's death in 1924. Wilson was one of the most thoughtful and articulate Christians of his day. He spoke with increasing perception and power on subjects ranging from problems of the ministry and Christian education to problems of the rural church in an urbanising society. He was, additionally, a pulpit preacher of moving eloquence and evangelical fervour. He preached only in the Princeton University Chapel, and all but one of his sermons have remained unpublished to this day. They were among the greatest speeches that he ever delivered and, it might be added, some of the greatest sermons of this century.[1]

Now, having established Wilson's religious credentials, so to speak, let us turn more directly to the subject of this paper and see how his religious inheritance from the Old World and his own additions to that inheritance influenced Woodrow Wilson as a politician and statesman.

III: MORALITY AND POLITICS

It is fairly common knowledge that Woodrow Wilson was an honourable man. His integrity was as considerable as his personal

---

[1] The following is an incomplete list of these papers, lectures and sermons: 'Religion and Patriotism', *Northfield* (Mass.) *Echoes*, IX (July 1902), pp. 217–21; *The Young People and the Church* (Philadelphia, 1905); *The Present Task of the Ministry* (Hartford, Conn., 1909); *The Ministry and the Individual* (Chicago, 1910); 'The Bible and Progress', *The Public Papers of Woodrow Wilson, College and State*, ed. by R. S. Baker and W. E. Dodd (New York, 2 vols., 1925), II, pp. 291–302; address to Trenton Sunday School assembly, 1 Oct. 1911, *Trenton True American*, 2 Oct. 1911; *The Minister and the Community* (New York, 1912); 'Militant Christianity', address before the Pittsburgh Y.M.C.A., 24 Oct. 1914, *The Public Papers of Woodrow Wilson, The New Democracy*, ed. by R. S. Baker and W. E. Dodd (New York, 2 vols., 1926), I, pp. 199–209; address before the Federal Council of the Churches of Christ in America, 10 Dec. 1915, ibid., pp. 429–45; address at his grandfather's church in Carlisle, England, 29 Dec. 1918, *The Public Papers of Woodrow Wilson, War and Peace*, ed. by R. S. Baker and W. E. Dodd (New York, 2 vols., 1927), I, pp. 347–8; 'The Road away from Revolution', ibid., II, pp. 536–9.

For Wilson's chapel talks and sermons, see the notes of chapel talks on 5 April 1891, 8 Nov. 1896, and 27 May 1900, and of talks before the Philadelphian Society, 2 Nov. 1899 and 20 Feb. 1902, all in the Papers of Woodrow Wilson, Library of Congress; baccalaureate addresses delivered on 12 June 1904 and 11 June 1905, ibid.; *The Free Life* (New York, 1908), Wilson's baccalaureate address in 1907; and baccalaureate addresses delivered on 7 June 1908 and 12 June 1910, MS in the Princeton University Library.

Extracts from and references to these writings and speeches will be made later in this paper without additional footnote references.

ethics were lofty. Before he entered politics he had already given abundant evidence of integrity as president of Princeton University in risking serious decline in enrolment by greatly elevating academic standards and refusing to change policies in order to please alumni or potential donors. He was the same kind of man in politics. He was incapable, not only of outright corruption, but also of more subtle and dangerous forms of corruption like acceptance of political support when he knew that strings were attached. For example, he nearly wrecked his chances for the presidential nomination in 1912 by literally telling the publisher William Randolph Hearst, whom he abhorred, to go to hell when Hearst offered to support Wilson's candidacy. He also resisted the most insidious temptation that can corrupt a leader in democracy, that of following policies simply because a majority of people seem to favour them. For example, he refused to yield to public clamour for a march through Germany in the autumn of 1918 and proceeded to negotiate for an end to the World War. And, when a senator warned him that he would be destroyed if he did not yield to public demand, he replied, 'So far as my being destroyed is concerned, I am willing if I can serve the country to go into a cellar and read poetry the remainder of my life. I am thinking now only of putting the U.S. into a position of strength and justice.'[1] More important, he refused later, in 1919–20, to accept the Lodge reservations to the Versailles Treaty and thereby made defeat of ratification inevitable, even though many of his friends, party leaders, and leaders of public opinion in the United States begged him to accept ratification on Lodge's terms. He simply could not do something that he believed constituted a rank betrayal of America's plighted word and stultification of his own creation, the League of Nations. There is no need to labour the obvious. Let it suffice to say that Wilson set an example of morality in politics excelled by few other statesmen in the modern world.

It is more important to talk about the wellspring of Wilson's morality. The initial source was the somewhat stern ethics that he inherited from Scottish and Scotch-Irish Presbyterianism by way of his family and Church. In Wilson's case, as in many others, adherence to a rigid moral code was sharpened and defined by the Calvinistic emphasis upon universal moral law and belief that men

---

[1] George F. Sparks (ed.), *A Many-Colored Toga, The Diary of Henry Fountain Ashurst* (Tucson, Ariz., 1963), p. 84.

and nations are moral agents accountable to God and transgress that law at the peril of divine judgement. This theme runs so strongly through all of Wilson's political speeches as to give the impression that he was simply a moraliser who lived rigidly by rules. His constant reference to what he called principles, and his occasional stubborn adherence to them, also suggest that Wilson had thoroughly imbibed the strong legalistic tradition of Scotland and Ireland.

Wilson certainly imbibed this tradition in his youth, but he also developed a much more advanced and sophisticated understanding of Christian ethics. He believed firmly, deeply, in moral law and judgement, but he came to understand them in the light of God's love and reconciling work in Jesus Christ. Moreover, he came to see that morality and character were by-products of obedience and to believe that Christ in the Holy Spirit alone gives men power to live righteously. He said these things many times, but nowhere more eloquently than in his baccalaureate sermon at Princeton University in 1905, as follows:

> And so the type and symbol is magnified,—Christ, the embodiment of great motive, of divine sympathy, of that perfect justice which seeks into the hearts of men, and that sweet grace of love which takes the sting out of every judgement.... He is the embodiment of those things which, not seen, are eternal,—the eternal force and grace and majesty, not of character, but of that which lies back of character, obedience to the informing will of the Father of our spirits. . . . [In Christ] we are made known to ourselves,—in him because he is God, and God is the end of our philosophy; the revelation of the thought which, if we will but obey it, shall make us free, lifting us to the planes where duty shall seem happiness, obedience liberty, life the fulfilment of the law.

Wilson suffered imperfection and mortality like the rest of men. He had a powerful ego and drive toward dominance. He had a tendency to identify his own solution with the moral law. He often sounded like a moraliser. But it is only fair to look at his entire career while coming to judgement about him. When one does this, the record shows a man committed very deeply to fundamental Christian affirmations about moral law, but also enormously flexible about details and methods, so long as they did not violate what he thought was right. He seems to have broken through the iron shell of Presbyterian legalism and come to an understanding of what is called contextual or relativistic ethics entirely on his own. However that may have been, one cannot truly know Wilson without concluding that here, indeed, was a man who tried to live by faith rather than rules in meeting complex moral problems in everyday life. As he put it in his baccalaureate sermon in 1905:

> But the standard? It is easy enough to talk of assessing moral values and of increasing the stock of good in the world, but what is good and what is evil, for us individually and for the world? May we not determine that deep question by our experience, candidly interrogated and interpreted,—by the peace, the ardour, the satisfaction our spirits get from our own days and their tasks,— by the tonic health we get from one course of action, the restlessness, the bitterness, the disappointment and weariness we get from another? . . . You shall not find happiness without health, and health lies in the constant rectification of the spirit, its love of the truth, its instinctive sincerity, its action without fear and without corruption of motive, its self-sufficing energy and independence. It is God's power in the heart. It is the spirit's consciousness of its immediate connection with his will and purpose. It is his saving health, which must be known among all nations before peace will come and life be widened in all its outlooks.

IV: GOD'S PROVIDENCE AND THE LORDSHIP OF JESUS CHRIST

Wilson was most heavily indebted to his Scottish and Scotch-Irish forbears in his emphasis upon the sovereignty and majesty of God. He literally stood in awe of the Almighty One. He was not a prig, and he sometimes used words which some Presbyterians would not approve. But using the Name lightly was to him blasphemy against divine majesty. His daughter, Mrs Eleanor Wilson McAdoo, has told the present speaker about his fearsome reaction when she once repeated a ditty that took liberties with God's name. This is mentioned merely as illustration of Wilson's consciousness, manifested in numerous other ways, that he stood constantly in the presence of a jealous God. He also inherited a rigorous Sabbatarianism from Scotch-Irish Presbyterianism through his family and Church. Like a devout Jew greeting the Sabbath he revelled in the joy of God's holy day. It was a time for reading, family worship, church attendance, and good works, not for labour or travel. Edith Bolling Wilson told the present

9

speaker about an embarrassing moment in Milan, when Wilson refused to attend an opera at La Scala on a Sunday evening. He went only when told that it would be a religious service.

This jealous God was, in Wilson's view, not only the Lord of individuals but also the Lord of history, ruler of men and nations, who turned all things to His own purpose. 'The idea of an all merciful God,' Wilson's brother-in-law, Stockton Axson, once said, 'was, I believe to him, a piece of soft sentimentality.' This did perhaps characterise Wilson's earlier understanding of God's sovereignty as it had been influenced by his Church's stern Calvinism and that of his professors when he was an undergraduate at Princeton. It was also Joseph Ruggles Wilson's view of God as expressed in his sermons, in so far as one can tell from the few that have survived. But the God that the son came to know through his father in conversation and correspondence was a different person. To be sure, He was the God of the Old Testament, because Joseph Ruggles Wilson, like most Presbyterians of his time, was not ardently Christological in theology. But in the father's view, God was also tender, loving, and merciful. Woodrow Wilson had shed most of the residue of scholastic, hardened Presbyterianism that remained in his own theology by the early 1900s. By this time he had come to the conviction that men know God truly only through Jesus Christ. God's saving work in history, he believed, is most clearly revealed in his work of reconciliation through Christ who is also the Lord of the Ages.

'The providence of God', Wilson told a Trenton, New Jersey, Sunday School convention in 1911, 'is the foundation of affairs.' Significantly, in the very next breath he linked providence to revelation, saying: 'Only those can guide, and only those can follow, who take this providence of God from the sources where it is authentically interpreted. . . . He alone can rule his own spirit who puts himself under the command of the Spirit of God, revealed in His Son, Jesus Christ, our Saviour. He is the captain of our souls; he is the man from whose suggestions and from whose life comes the light that guideth every man that came into the world.'

About the irresistibility of God's providential work, another Calvinistic theme inherited from his forbears, Wilson had the following to say in a famous address on the Bible, delivered in Denver, Colorado, in 1911:

The man whose faith is rooted in the Bible knows that reform cannot be stayed, that the finger of God that moves upon the face of the nations is against every man that plots the nation's downfall or the people's deceit; that these men are simply groping and staggering in their ignorance to a fearful day of judgement; and that whether one generation witnesses it or not the glad day of revelation and of freedom will come in which men will sing by the host of the coming of the Lord in His glory, and all of those will be forgotten—those little, scheming, contemptible creatures that forgot the image of God and tried to frame men according to the image of the evil one.

There was power in faith such as this. For Wilson it provided, when plans were succeeding, the strength and joy that come from conviction that one is doing God's work in the world. It also brought courage and hope in the time of his greatest adversity and sorrow, when the Senate wrecked his work at Versailles and, as he believed, the best hope for peace in the world. 'I feel like going to bed and staying there,' he told his physician, Doctor Cary T. Grayson, after he had received word that the Senate had rejected the treaty for a second time. But later in the night he asked Doctor Grayson to read the marvellous words of Second Corinthians 4: 8–9: 'We are troubled on every side, yet not distressed; we are perplexed, but not in despair; persecuted, but not forsaken; cast down, but not destroyed.' Then Wilson said, 'If I were not a Christian, I think I should go mad, but my faith in God holds me to the belief that He is some way working out His own plans through human perversities and mistakes.'[1]

To be sure, faith like this carried obvious dangers, the principal one being the temptation to believe that what the self wants to do is what God commands, and that one's opponents are not only mistaken but also of evil heart and mind. It was a particularly acute danger for a person of Wilson's highly combative personality. He often said that he had inherited this trait from his Scotch-Irish ancestors. He might have added his Presbyterian kinsmen both in the Old World and the New, who were eternally fighting among themselves. In any event, Wilson loved nothing better than an intellectual duel or oratorical contest. He always insisted that he abhorred personal controversy. Perhaps he did, but he was drawn into such fights from time to time, and, once

[1] Cary T. Grayson, *Woodrow Wilson, An Intimate Memoir* (New York, 1960), p. 106.

engaged, he could give as well as take. Wilson also became entangled in political controversy because of his deep commitment to fundamental principles. Some of the reasons for this passion for principles may have been personal stubbornness, pride, egotism, and a tendency to identify subjective conclusions with objectively right principles. All these factors certainly contributed to his inflexibility to a varying degree. But they alone do not account for his passionate convictions. He, at any rate, believed that they stemmed from the innermost resources of Christian faith, in other words, that they were given. Wilson, having received them, was as bound by them as anyone else, even more bound by them. They were the imperatives of his life. He could not be false to them without betraying God. Another trait that led Wilson into controversy was his unrelenting will, his absolute determination to accomplish objectives that he believed were right. Once again, his motives were no doubt mixed. His will was fired by pride, the egotistical belief that he knew better than others, and the ambition for fame and glory. But it was fired more often by an urgent, compelling sense of duty and destiny that would not let him go and drove him on and on in spite of insuperable odds. The destiny that he saw for himself was in many respects terrible, for in the end it led to his physical destruction. But he believed that he could not turn his back upon it because it was the destiny marked out by the sovereign God of history.

And yet it must be said that all leaders who stand and fight for great causes have to run all these risks. And if Wilson succumbed at times to pride and wilful egotism, he never forgot for long that he was a servant of Jesus Christ, and that final judgement belongs to God. As he once said in a reflective moment about men with whom he disagreed, 'While we are going to judge with the absolute standard of righteousness, we are going to judge with Christian feeling, being men of a like sort ourselves, suffering the same temptations, having the same weaknesses, knowing the same passions; and while we do not condemn, we are going to seek to say and to live the truth.'[1]

V: PRESBYTERIANISM AND AN ORDERED POLITICAL SYSTEM

Woodrow Wilson knew the polity, laws and procedures of the Presbyterian Church long before he knew those of his state and

[1] In his address before the Pittsburgh Y.M.C.A., 24 Oct. 1914.

nation. Thus it is a temptation, particularly to an admirer and practitioner of the Presbyterian form of government, to say that Wilson was profoundly influenced by the constitutional structure and political ethos of the Presbyterian Church. The influence operated, and operated undoubtedly in a powerful way. The trouble in talking about it is that it was indirect and cannot be seen as precisely, for example, as Walter Bagehot's influence on Wilson's ideas about the proper form of parliamentary organisation. But we are not totally in the dark, and I think that we are entitled to say that the experience of growing up in the Presbyterian Church influenced Wilson's more general secular political ideology at least in the following ways:

First, it caused him from his youth to have a passion for orderly representative government, for doing political business in a decent way. There is a story that his first constitution was one that he drafted while a boy in Augusta for a baseball association called the 'Lightfoot Club'. This may be mythological. The first Wilsonian written constitution that has survived is the one that he drafted in the summer of 1874 for an imaginative 'Royal United Kingdom Yacht Club'. Then followed a constitution for the Liberal Debating Club, which Wilson organised at Princeton in 1877; a new constitution for the Jefferson Literary Society at the University of Virginia in 1880; a new constitution for the Hopkins Literary Society, re-named the Hopkins House of Commons, in 1884; a constitution for the Wesleyan House of Commons at Wesleyan University in 1889; and so on down through the Covenant of the League of Nations. The form of government established by these constitutions varied, but all of them demonstrated Wilson's concern for orderly representative government and for making it work.

Second, Wilson inherited from the Calvinistic tradition its repudiation of the rationale of an ordered society based upon birth or wealth. With Wilson it was an inherited assumption that God is no respecter of persons and calls whom He will to bear rule in Church and State. This was Calvinism's most important contribution to modern political development. In the case of the United States, it was one of the main causes for the development of what would eventually become equalitarian democracy. In Wilson's own case, it was the foundation stone of an unchanging belief in the inherent capacity of all men, generally speaking, for self-government.

Third, Wilson inherited from Scottish and Scotch-Irish

Presbyterianism its basic conservatism along with its fundamental equalitarianism. The most important ingredient of this conservatism was the belief in God's sovereignty over the historical process. Men may propose, but God disposes in the end. The second ingredient was belief in election and what it implies by way of responsibility. Hence emphasis upon education. The third ingredient was belief in original sin. All of mankind's works are infected with imperfection and death. These were all fundamental beliefs with Woodrow Wilson, and they shaped and controlled his thinking about the way historical change occurs, the limited possibilities of human progress, and the unlimited power of God to achieve His ends in history.

VI: CHRISTIANITY, SOCIAL CONSCIENCE AND POLITICAL ACTION

The most remarkable thing about Wilson as a political leader was the change that occurred in his thinking about the functions of government. Even more remarkable was the way Wilson's views on government paralleled his thinking about the Christian's duty toward fellow-man.

Wilson grew up during the high tide of individualism in the western world. His political heroes were the English and Scottish devotees of *laissez faire*; his economic mentors, British and American classical economists. He inherited from scholastic Presbyterianism, both American and Scottish, its pietism, individualism, and almost total rejection of organised social action either by religious or political communities. He seems to have been oblivious of the great movement to reawaken Christian social conscience that began in an organised way in the 1860s and was beginning to leaven religious thought and life by the 1890s. This was true of Wilson even as late as the first decade of the twentieth century. He gained what little political fame he then enjoyed as a critic of the American reformers, William J. Bryan and Theodore Roosevelt, and as an advocate of very cautious solutions of economic and political problems.

Wilson's political thought first began to show signs of changing about 1907, and the first sign of this metamorphosis was a significant shift in his thinking about the role that Christians and the Church should play in the world at large. He delivered three major addresses on this subject between 1906 and 1909—'The Minister

and the Community', in 1906, and 'The Present Task of the
Ministry' and 'The Ministry and the Individual', both in 1909.
They revealed that Wilson had not yet altogether shed his earlier
pietism and intense individualism. The Church's duty, he said, was
to save individual souls. Christ was not a social reformer. As he
put it, 'Christianity, come what may, must be fundamentally and
forever individualistic.' The minister should 'preach Christianity
to men, not to society. He must preach salvation to the individual.'

Yet we can see a momentous intellectual ferment clearly
reflected in the last two lectures. We find Wilson also saying in
1909 that 'If men cannot lift their fellow-men in the process of
saving themselves, I do not see that it is very important that they
should save themselves. . . . Christianity came into the world to
save the world as well as to save individual men, and individual
men can afford in conscience to be saved only as part of the
process by which the world itself is regenerated.'

Wilson's movement into the ranks of advanced reform after he
entered politics in 1910 is well known. From the beginning of his
political career he was in the forefront of the fight to overhaul the
American political institutional structure. During the first two or
three years of his presidency he also fought for fundamental
changes in national economic policies. But he was notably reluc-
tant before 1916 to support or even countenance what might be
called advanced social reform, that is, legislation for the protection
and welfare of disadvantaged groups, at least when such legislation involved the direct intervention of the Federal government
in economic and social life.

Wilson crossed his political Rubicon in 1916 by espousing
and winning adoption of a series of measures, including the first
Federal child-labour law, one that put national government
squarely into the business of social amelioration for the first time.
Moreover, he went on during the presidential campaign of 1916
to describe his vision of the new good society in which government would be ceaselessly at work to restrain exploiters, uplift the
downtrodden, protect women and children, and defend the help-
less and weak. It was nothing less than a vision of the modern
welfare state. Again, the significant fact about his vision was its
origin, at least in part, in Wilson's Christian social conscience.
The awakening, if such it may be called, was caused by Wilson's
own broadening political experiences and the social gospel, which

was then running at high tide in American Protestanism. It was derived only very indirectly from his more particular Presbyterian inheritance.

VII: AMERICA'S MISSION TO THE WORLD AS MINISTRY

Woodrow Wilson's whole thinking about foreign policy was shaped by his concept of ministry and his belief in divine providence. Ministry, as he said many times, is Christ's ministry of unselfish service to individuals, societies and nations. He believed that God had created the United States out of diverse peoples for a specific, eschatological role in history—as one scholar has written, 'to realise an ideal of liberty, provide a model of democracy, vindicate moral principles, give examples of action and ideals of government and righteousness to an interdependent world, uphold the rights of man, work for humanity and the happiness of men everywhere, lead the thinking of the world, promote peace,—in sum, to serve mankind and progress.'[1] Hence foreign policy should not be used for material ends, not even defined in terms of material interests. America's mission in the world was not to attain wealth and power, but to fulfil God's plan by unselfish service to mankind.

These beliefs were all, in their fundamentals, the inheritance of an activistic Calvinism brought to the New World by English Puritans and Scottish and Scotch-Irish Presbyterians. They were also greatly affected by the ecumenical, world-wide missionary movement of the early twentieth century in which Wilson participated as a member of the Presbyterian Church and of the World Student Movement of the Y.M.C.A. Wilson came to the presidency in 1913, as has often been noted, with no training and very little interest in the practical details of foreign affairs and diplomacy. Naturally, inevitably, he simply adopted all his assumptions about the nature of the Church's world-wide ministry as the controlling assumptions of his foreign policy. And during his first two years in the White House, he and his first Secretary of State, William J. Bryan, another Presbyterian elder who shared Wilson's motivation, put into force what has been called 'missionary diplomacy' aimed at helping underdeveloped countries work toward domestic order and democracy.

[1] Harley Notter, *The Origins of the Foreign Policy of Woodrow Wilson* (Baltimore, 1937), p. 653.

Wilson soon discovered that a diplomacy of helpfulness was immensely difficult, troublesome and dangerous. He soon learned that it was not always possible to impose even altruistic solutions on other countries. Experience rapidly dispelled Wilson's naïveté. The hopeful, eager diplomatist became the Christian realist, doing what he could in the knowledge that ideal solutions were not always possible. But Wilson's basic motivation and objectives never changed. He struggled to avoid involvement in the First World War in part because he ardently desired to use American power for a noble purpose—mediation of the conflict. He accepted belligerency in 1917 in large part because he then believed that American participation was now the surest if not the only way to lasting peace. He created the League of Nations in part because he thought that it would be the instrument of America's redemptive work in the world. And he spent his health and strength in trying to convince Americans that God had laid the burdens of leadership for peace on them. As he said when he presented the Versailles Treaty to the Senate on 10 July 1919: 'The stage is set, the destiny disclosed. It has come about by no plan of our conceiving, but by the hand of God who led us into this way. We cannot turn back. We can only go forward, with lifted eyes and freshened spirit, to follow the vision. It was of this that we dreamed at our birth. America shall in truth show the way. The light streams upon the path ahead, and nowhere else.'[1]

This paper began with Woodrow Wilson's Scottish and Scotch-Irish inheritance of family and religious traditions. It explored Wilson's own Christian faith and tried to demonstrate that it stemmed essentially from Calvinistic, Presbyterian formulations and affirmations and was the source and motivation of all his thinking about ethics, political and social action, and America's role in the world at large. This discussion has also tried to show how developments, or new emphases, in American Presbyterianism and Protestantism and his own broadening experiences led Wilson into new understanding of the meaning of Christian faith in changing circumstances. If there be any justification for such a lecture to such an audience as this one, it is that in Woodrow Wilson we see almost perfectly revealed the signal Scottish and Scotch-Irish legacy to American society, culture and politics.

[1] *The Public Papers of Woodrow Wilson, War and Peace,* I, pp. 551–2.

CHAPTER II

Education in the American Colonies: The Impact of Scotland

by Esmond Wright

The history of emigration from Scotland is fully and properly charged with deep emotion: its songs and much of its folklore tell of the sadness of journeys that could never count on a return; emigration usually equalled exile; the lone shieling and the misty island are part of that vivid imagery of Scotland that the exile carried with him to places as far apart as the Fraser River of British Columbia and Perth in Western Australia. Earlier on he had carried them with him—but lost them—in service in Russian and French armies. That many of the seventeenth- and eighteenth-century emigrants went first to Northern Ireland adds further to the poignancy: their American exile was often exile for a second time. And at the ultimate receiving end, the story of the American immigrant is of a different pride: pride in the achievements that the New World made possible, and a quest for roots that, as also with Australians, often brought in its train curious and un-expected and occasionally unwelcome discoveries. The history of folk movements is a fascinating and rich subject. The story of the ideas that were carried with the migrants is equally fascinating and even more complex to disentangle.[1]

[1] There is a vast literature on emigration and immigration. Major studies include: Carl Wittke, *We Who Built America, The Saga of the Immigrant* (New York, 1939); Marcus L. Hansen, *The Atlantic Migration, 1607–1860. A History of the Continuing Settlement of the United States* (Cambridge, Mass., 1940); Oscar Handlin (ed.), *Immigration as a Factor in American History* (Englewood Cliffs, New Jersey, 1959); Maldwyn A. Jones, *American Immigration* (Chicago, 1960); H. S. Commager (ed.), *Immigration and American History* (Minneapolis, 1961).

Throughout the eighteenth century many colonial records describe immigrants from Ireland simply as 'Irish'. Despite Edmund Burke's reference to those 'who in America are generally called Scotch-Irish' and Thomas Jefferson's similar use of the phrase to describe no less a person than himself, the term 'Scotch-Irish' was in fact not yet in general use. Lord Adam Gordon, however, found Winchester, Virginia in 1760 'inhabited by a spurious race of mortals known by the appellation of Scotch-Irish'. Woodmason in North Carolina refers to 'the herd of vile Irish Presbyterians'. These groups were usually referred to as simply Irish. And some Irish and Irish-American historians have done their best to blur the distinction: to argue that a century of residence in Ireland made all emigrants Irish, that much inter-marriage occurred between native Irish women and Ulster Scots, and that because of the proscription that obtained against the Roman Catholic religion in many English colonies, many described as Protestants were Irish Catholics in disguise. All true Americans in this view have lots of cousins in County Wexford. What is, however, clearly established is that there were few avowed Catholics in the American colonies before the Revolution: Bishop Carroll reported to the Vatican in 1785 that there were 18,000 (of whom 16,000 were in Maryland, 1,500 in New York, 700 in Pennsylvania and 200 in Virginia) out of a total population of about 3 million. The leading student of colonial religious history, W. W. Sweet, puts the figure at 24,000, but this included, of course, many—perhaps a majority—who came from countries other than Ireland, especially Germany and France. The Southern Irish contribution before the Revolution seems, on the whole, to have been small.[1]

Three valuable studies of the Scotch-Irish are: C. A. Hanna, *The Scotch-Irish* (New York, 1902); Henry J. Ford, *The Scotch-Irish in America* (Princeton, 1915); and Ian C. C. Graham, *Colonists from Scotland: Emigration to North America 1707–1783* (Ithaca, 1956). There is also useful material in A. L. Perry, *Scotch-Irish in New England* (Boston, 1891); and C. K. Bolton, *Scotch-Irish Pioneers in Ulster and America* (Boston, 1910).

And for the eighteenth-century intellectual background, two studies are indispensable: Michael Kraus, *The Atlantic Civilization—Eighteenth Century Origins* (Ithaca, 1949); and Caroline Robbins, *The Eighteenth-Century Commonwealthman* (Cambridge, 1961).

[1] Richard S. Hooker (ed.), *The Carolina Back-Country on the Eve of the Revolution: The Journal and other Writings of Charles Woodmason, Anglican Itinerant* (Chapel Hill, 1953). Duane Meyer, *The Highland Scots of North Carolina 1732–76* (Chapel Hill, 1957).

Education in the American Colonies

Moreover, however widely used the generic term 'Irish' might be, as early as 1720 the Scotch-Irish in the colonies were coming to resent it. The inhabitants of Londonderry, New Hampshire, expressed their surprise in 1720 at being described as 'Irish people', 'when we so frequently ventured our all for the British Crown and Liberties against the Irish Papists'. However unfamiliar to us in the Old World—and the term Scotch-Irish has puzzled even Professors of Scottish History in Glasgow in recent years—it is the familiar term in the New: it distinguishes all those Scots who moved to America or whose ancestors moved to America after a period of residence, long or short, in Ulster.[1]

The people of Ulster retained in the New World something of the distinctiveness they had in the Old. They maintained their Protestantism, their hatred for Catholicism and their contempt for the 'mere Irish'. They had always described themselves as 'the Scottish nation in the north of Ireland'. Francis Makemie, the Ulster Scot who was the principal founder of the Presbyterian Church in America, is entered on the matriculation register of Glasgow University as Scoto Hibernus, a Scot of Ireland. And to a striking extent they never became hyphenated Americans. One speaks of Irish-Americans, German-Americans, Italian-Americans and Polish-Americans, the hyphen testifying to a dual allegiance, but never of Scottish-Americans, and always simply of the Scotch-Irish. And the adjective is proudly Scotch, not Scots or Scottish —even if the word 'Scotch' also, of course, serves as a noun. One notes Professor Galbraith's views of his own boyhood in Canada, when he says

> Nearly everyone in our part of the world was Scotch. Certainly it never occurred to us that a well-regulated community could be populated by any other kind of people. We referred to ourselves as Scotch and not Scots. When, years later, I learned that the usage in Scotland was different, it seemed to me rather an affectation. . . .
> Our Scotch neighbours might be tall or short, stocky or lean,

Michael J. O'Brien, *A Hidden Phase of American History, Ireland's Part in America's Struggle for Liberty* (New York, 1919).

W. F. Dunaway, *A History of Pennsylvania* (Philadelphia, 1935).

— *The Scotch-Irish of Colonial Pennsylvania* (Philadelphia, 1944).

W. W. Sweet, *Religion in Colonial America* (New York, 1942).

Graham, op. cit.

Pennsylvania Scotch-Irish Society, *Proceedings, passim.*

[1] See George S. Pryde, *The Scottish Universities and the Colleges of Colonial America* (Glasgow, 1957), p. 3, and *passim.*

although most of them were unremarkably in between. But it was evident at a glance that they were made to last. Their faces and hands were covered not with a pink or white film but a heavy, red parchment designed to give protection in extremes of climate for a lifetime. It had the appearance of leather, and appearances were not deceptive. This excellent material was stretched over a firm bony structure on which the nose was by all odds the most prominent feature. Additional protection, though it may not have been absolutely essential, was provided for most of the week by a stiff-bristled beard. The story was told in my youth of a stranger who, in a moment of aberration, poked one of the McKillop boys on the jaw. He would not have been more damaged, it was said, if he had driven his fist into a roll of barbed wire. In any case, he was badly wounded.[1]

It is relatively easy to dissect the various strands in the Scottish migration: Highland communities in Albany, New York, and Cape Fear, North Carolina; individual Lowlanders; men on the make in the tidewater; Scotch-Irish in New Jersey, in Western Pennsylvania and in the Valley of Virginia. It is much less easy to be specific about their intellectual contributions. The records of ship movements, of port entries, of land holdings are clearer than the records of ideas and of educational influences. Broadly, the Scots on the coast were Loyalist, and in 1776 many left, never to return. Broadly, the Cape Fear Highlanders in North Carolina were Loyalist too, to be destroyed as they crossed Moore's Creek Bridge in 1776—destroyed in part because the timbers of the bridge had been removed and the girders greased and they were easy targets as they tried to clamber across. Broadly, the Scotch-Irish on the frontier were patriots. At King's Mountain, North Carolina, in 1780 the Revolutionary War largely took the form of Scot *versus* Scotch-Irish. And the Scotch-Irish defeated the Highlanders whom Colonel Patrick Ferguson was seeking to organise for Lord Cornwallis and George III. The Ulster Scots constituted the very back-bone of Washington's army. To Henry Lee the line of Pennsylvania 'might as well be called "the line of Ireland"'.

In equally broad terms it can be said that the Scotch-Irish made three contributions to colonial America: they settled the frontier, they founded the Kirk, and they built the school. They, more than

[1] John K. Galbraith, *Made To Last* (London, 1964), pp. 18, 20–1.

any other group, created the first western frontier. Frontiers there had, of course, been before in history, but not frontiers cut off from water communication with Europe, as were those of western Pennsylvania and the southern back country. And few countries were so quickly settled. The westward movement was one marked not merely by the movement of men but by the movement of little red schoolhouses and tall white spires. To the Ulster Scots must largely go the credit of being the first pioneers west of the Appalachians and of opening the Mississippi valley to British civilisation. It was not only distant but distinct from Tidewater, and out of tune with it. J. T. Adams in his *The Epic of America* describes a tombstone over the grave of a Scotch-Irish pioneer in the Shenandoah Valley—a perfect epitome of the history of many a Scotch-Irish group:

> Here lies the remains of John Lewis, who slew the Irish lord, settled in Augusta County, located the town of Staunton, and furnished five sons to fight the battles of the American Revolution.

They brought Presbyterianism too, as did the tidewater Scots. The frontier was so thinly populated that it was difficult to organise congregations and to secure ministers to serve them. Appeals for ministers for the aptly named 'desolate places' poured in to Scottish and Irish presbyteries and synods. Few responded. The solution was found in the circuit-rider, even if such a Methodist term would have been horrifying to them. Armed with the Bible, and with their meagre belongings packed in saddle-bags, youthful clergymen rode from community to community along the frontier, holding services often in barns, often in the open. In time, however, little churches, constructed of logs, were built in the forest clearings. Before the end of the eighteenth century there were hundreds of Presbyterian congregations dotting the great region from the Susquehanna in Pennsylvania to northern Georgia. By 1763 all the colonies except Rhode Island had a Presbyterian church or churches—Presbyterianism was, from the start, a factor making for federalism. And one of the principal events determining the colonies on resistance to the Crown was the issue in May 1775 of a Pastoral Letter by the General Synod of the Presbyterian Church in Philadelphia.

Presbyterianism left a decisive mark. As the Rev. H. D. Lindsey put it as late as 1913:

Pittsburgh is Presbyterian through and through. Its very smoke has a bluish tinge. The man you meet on the street is a Presbyterian, and if not a Presbyterian he is a United Presbyterian, and if he is not a United Presbyterian he is an Associated Presbyterian, and if not an Associated Presbyterian he is a Reformed Presbyterian, and if you have missed it all along the line he hastens to assure you that his father is a Covenanter.[1]

Moreover, on the western frontier ministers had to be men of parts, men like John Elder. A native of County Antrim and a graduate of the University of Edinburgh, he was pastor of the Presbyterian church at Derry in western Pennsylvania from 1738 to 1791, and for a time of Paxtang—the place from which the Paxton Boys marched in 1764, to horrify the douce Quakers of Philadelphia. When John Elder entered the pulpit he carried his rifle with him up the winding stairs and kept it close beside him; the men in his congregation stacked theirs under guard at the entrance to the church, or hung them on the wooden pins provided around the interior of the building. The Reverend John Steel, another of the fighting parsons, was pastor of the church at Mercersburg, and also of the churches at Greencastle and Carlisle, in the Cumberland Valley. On one occasion he led a band of a hundred men against the Indians.

These men, too, were educators. Thaddeus Dod, graduate of Princeton, long a pastor on the frontier, founded Washington Academy in 1787. And John McMillan, another Princeton graduate was active in the Redstone country of western Pennsylvania and in Kentucky and Tennessee. He died in 1833 aged 81. He was perhaps as typical of the frontier as any. He and the Reverend Joseph Patterson, on their way to attend a meeting of the Presbytery at Pittsburgh, stopped at an inn to refresh themselves. Two glasses of whisky were set down and Dr McMillan proposed a prayer and a blessing. Patterson's blessing was protracted and McMillan, putting forth his hand, drained off first one glass and then the other. When the prayer was finally ended and Patterson, opening his expectant eyes, saw only two empty glasses, McMillan said to him, 'My brother, on the frontier you must watch as well as pray.'[2]

And they brought not only the Kirk but the school. As among the other racial groups of the provinces, the typical elementary

[1] Quoted in Dunaway, *Scotch-Irish*, pp. 205–6.   [2] Ibid., p. 216.

23

school among the Scotch-Irish was the church school. Little was taught in these schools beyond the rudiments—reading, writing, arithmetic and spelling. The Bible was the usual daily reader, and the Shorter Catechism was recited by all the school every Saturday morning. The equipment of these early schools was very meagre—they were rough log-cabins, with benches and tables made of spilt logs. Pens were made of goose quills, but there were no blackboards, slates, or pencils. In the beginning the log churches served also as schoolhouses, but as stability and prosperity came better church buildings were erected and new buildings were then constructed to be used as schoolhouses. However primitive the provision, the principle was clear. In the colonies, as at home, a learned ministry was the cornerstone of Presbyterianism.

The first of the schools of higher grade to be established in Pennsylvania by the Scotch-Irish was the celebrated 'Log College' founded by the Reverend William Tennent, Sr, at Neshaminy, twenty miles north of Philadelphia. This school was the first institution founded by American Presbyterians designed to educate young men for the ministry. Its founder was Irish born, a cousin of James Logan, a graduate of Edinburgh in 1695 and a minister in the Established Church of Ireland. He became dissatisfied either because he was unable to find a parish, or because of the growing Arminianism of that Establishment. He emigrated in 1716 with wife and four sons and two years later applied for admission to the Presbyterian Synod of Philadelphia. He became pastor of the Presbyterian church at Neshaminy in 1726, and here continued until his death in 1746. His school, twenty feet square, was built on a fifty-acre tract given him by his cousin; it was founded in 1726 or 1727, and survived until 1742. George Whitefield, who visited the school in 1739, says: 'The place wherein the young men study is in contempt called the College. It is a log-house, about twenty feet long, and near as many broad; and to me it seemed to resemble the schools of the prophets. . . .' It was not in any sense a college (it had no Charter and gave no degrees) but an academy in which Greek, Latin and the 'arts and sciences' were taught, along with theology. He taught all the classes himself, and preached on Sunday; and he earned the title of 'Hell-fire' Tennent. He and his son Gilbert were leaders in the Great Awakening, and revivalists with a Whitefield flavour who gave Presbyterianism its New Side or New Light character. One Bostonian, describing a 'revival' wrote:

> There is a Creature here which you perhaps never heard of before. It is called *an Exhorter*. It is of both sexes, but generally of the male, and young. Its distinguishing qualities are ignorance, impudence, zeal. . . . Such of them as have good voices do *great Execution*; they move their hearers, make them cry, faint, swoon, fall into convulsions. . . . You may hear screaming, singing, laughing, praying, all at once; and, in other parts, they fall into visions, trances, convulsions. When they come out of their trances, they commonly tell a senseless story of Heaven and Hell, and whom and what they saw there.[1]

It is not surprising perhaps that the examining synod found some of his products deficient in theology and some branches of learning. The College, which was supported entirely on fees paid by its students, had distinguished alumni: three of Tennent's own sons and Samuel Blair, John Blair, Samuel Finley, Charles Beatty and John Rowland, of whom a number became themselves educators. John Blair and Samuel Finley became presidents of Princeton; in fact, the Log College was the germ from which Princeton developed. They were the noted preachers of the next generation and themselves founders of academies. The Reverend Samuel Blair founded Fagg's Manor Classical School in Chester County in 1739, with its own distinguished group of graduates. Samuel Finley, who was born in County Armagh in Ireland, established Nottingham Academy before going on to Princeton. By the end of the century Presbyterian ministers founded some 100 schools.

A very different type of school was founded by the Presbyterians in the Scotch-Irish settlement at New London. This school, known as the New London Academy, grew out of the academy founded by Dr Francis Alison in 1744. Dr Alison, a native of County Donegal, Ireland, was educated at the University of Glasgow. Around 1735 he emigrated to Pennsylvania at the age of thirty and became a tutor in the home of Samuel Dickinson, the father of John Dickinson, where he taught the future author of the *Farmer's Letters*, along with several other boys. In 1737 he became pastor of the Presbyterian church at New London, where

[1] W. W. Sweet, *Religion in Colonial America* (New York, 1953), p. 285.

he bought a farm and started a school, which was at first a purely private enterprise. Among its alumni were John Ewing, James Latta and Matthew Wilson, ministers; Charles Thomson, later to be Secretary of the Continental Congress; Hugh Williamson and David Ramsay, historians of North Carolina and South Carolina respectively; and Thomas McKean, James Smith and George Read, signers of the Declaration of Independence. In 1743 the Synod of Philadelphia began to consider the advisability of establishing under ecclesiastical control a school for the education of ministers and in the following year approved a plan for this purpose. Dr Alison's school was chosen as the one best suited to the requirements of the Synod, and it was agreed to take it under control. The agreement provided that free instruction should be afforded 'in the Languages, Philosophy and Divinity to all who chose to attend', and that the school should be supported by contributions from the churches composing the Synod. This arrangement continued from 1744 to 1752, when Dr Alison removed to Philadelphia to assume charge of the academy connected with the College of Philadelphia, where he became vice-provost and professor of moral philosophy in 1755. After his removal, the Reverend Alexander McDowell was placed in charge of the school at New London. How long the Synod continued to support McDowell is not clear, though probably not beyond 1758, in which year Princeton became the authorised school of the Synod and thereafter the recipient of the funds for the education of Presbyterian young men entering the ministry. Princeton and Yale conferred upon Alison the degree of A.M., and the University of Glasgow conferred on him the degree of D.D. He was the first American to be so honoured by a European university. As these names suggest, the Scotch-Irish Academy and its product dominated the next generation and was one reason why, by the 1750s, the Scotch-Irish took over the Quaker 'party' and made it by 1776 the dominant group in the state—a democratic force from which the highly radical State Constitution of 1776 came.[1]

The Scotch-Irish were also particularly strong in the Cumberland Valley—they established here Dickinson College at Carlisle,

[1] James Mulhern, *A History of Secondary Education in Pennsylvania* (Philadelphia, 1933).
  T. J. Wertenbaker, *Princeton 1746–1896* (Princeton, 1946).
  T. H. Montgomery, *A History of the University of Pennsylvania from its Foundations to A.D. 1770* (Philadelphia, 1900).

the first denominational college in Pennsylvania and the twelfth college to be founded in the United States. While the College of Philadelphia was theoretically non-sectarian, the dominant influence in its board of trustees and faculty had become Episcopalian, a circumstance which irked the Presbyterians and led them to desire a college of their own. Though the dominant influence behind the founding of Dickinson College in 1783 was that of the Scotch-Irish Presbyterians, the enlarged aims of its founders enlisted the support of public-spirited men like Dr Benjamin Rush and John Dickinson.

But of these schools, one was decisively important, Princeton—decisively Presbyterian and Scottish in character, virtually a foster-child of Scotland. The aim of the college was to provide a non-denominational higher education, in which ministerial training, however prominent, would be incidental; and the charter guaranteed 'free and equal liberty and advantage of education' to persons of all sects. And other elements had their place. Yale was to some extent the model as regards instruction and textbooks; and the English dissenting academies, with their pronounced trend towards the natural sciences, as well as their evangelical tone, were a source of inspiration for the early presidents of the college. But the college languished for twenty years under five presidents, whose short incumbencies were a prime cause of weakness. Of these the first three, Jonathan Dickinson, Aaron Burr and Jonathan Edwards, were New Englanders and Yale graduates, while the next two, Samuel Davies and Samuel Finley, were 'Log College men'; stability and, with it, renown came only under the sixth president, John Witherspoon.

Born at Gifford in 1723, Witherspoon was educated at Haddington grammar school and Edinburgh University, where the greatest influence was exercised upon him (as upon his contemporary, Hugh Blair) by John Stevenson, professor of logic (which then included rhetoric). Ordained to Beith in 1745 and transferred to Paisley in 1757, he aligned himself with the Evangelical party in the Church, and became known as the author of a popular skit on the Moderates, wherein their lack of piety, 'mere morality', secular learning and tolerance of patronage were attacked. It was as an outspoken and orthodox ecclesiastical leader that he was invited to take the headship of the College of New Jersey in 1766; he refused, but was persuaded (largely through the counsels of the

27

young Princeton graduate, Benjamin Rush, then studying medicine at Edinburgh) to accept the offer, and was inaugurated in August 1768. His wife had taken even more persuading. Every time her husband spoke of crossing the Atlantic she had hysterics and took to her bed. Young Billy Patterson, a future Associate Justice of the Supreme Court, wrote to his chum John McPherson —'Witherspoon is President. Mercy on me! We shall be overrun with Scotchmen, the worst vermin under heaven.'

Witherspoon's long reign (1768–94) was decisive for Princeton: by shrewd, forceful and inspiring leadership, he was able to realise those noble ideals which, before his arrival, seemed to be beyond the moral and spiritual resources of native American Presbyterianism. His experiences in Scottish ecclesiastical politics gave him the knowledge and confidence to apply the lessons which he had imbibed from his seven years' arts-and-divinity course at Edinburgh. The impact of his vigorous personality was immediately apparent. Not that the basis of the curriculum, already wide under his predecessors, was materially changed. Freshmen studied Latin, Greek and rhetoric, as they had before; sophomores continued with languages and took up geography and the elements of philosophy and mathematics; juniors were concerned mainly with mathematics and natural philosophy; and seniors had advanced courses in these two branches, in classics and in moral philosophy. The president himself gave additional lectures to the higher classes in chronology and history, composition and criticism. If there is little formal difference between the curricula of 1764 and 1772, nevertheless 1768 provides a sharp dividing-line: the stirring of new life from that very year is undeniable. At his first meeting with his board, Witherspoon announced gifts from overseas of some 300 volumes for the library. Another of his very early measures concerned the teaching of French. To revitalise the grammar school at Nassau hall, so that it could serve as a feeder for the college, he introduced the 'book of directions' and the 'pedagogical method' used at Glasgow High School. LL.D.s were being conferred from 1769, D.D.s from 1770. From 1771, moreover, thanks to such purchases as that of the celebrated Rittenhouse orrery, the College was acquiring a sound reputation in experimental and natural science. At the same time, English grammar and composition, together with literary style, taste and fluency, were cultivated more diligently under Witherspoon than under his forerunners, and the typically Scottish emphasis on lectures, in preference to disputations and frequent tests or 'quizzes', is noteworthy.

It was, however, in two other and major respects that Witherspoon's innovations, or shifts of direction, bore the most abundant fruit. In the first place, the philosophy which he taught, sponsored and tolerated to the exclusion of any rival form, was derived from Hutcheson, Reid and the 'Common Sense' school and was opposed alike to Berkeley's idealism, to Hume's scepticism, and to all shades of materialism, rationalism and deism. Accepting as facts 'immediate cognition and . . . direct knowledge of real qualities in things and the unchangeable relations between them', Witherspoon insisted that 'Scotch-American realism' was the natural and the national philosophy, and implied that other systems were, in effect, 'un-American'. Rigid, conservative and almost overbearing, he imposed his ideas in an authoritarian manner on his own college, suppressed the competing systems, and sent forth missionaries who conquered the south and the west and battled effectively with New England transcendentalism. The victory of 'common sense' was so nearly complete as to involve some 'loss of a . . . spirit of liberality' and of speculation.

In the second place—and as a matter of yet greater moment— Witherspoon inculcated the ideals of patriotism, nationality and public service. Despite his theological training and evangelical temper, he found himself, as a teacher of philosophy, history and rhetoric, more and more embroiled in secular affairs. The essential character of his college was markedly changed. It became 'a school of very practical politics', producing 'more men of affairs than men of the cloth': in the twenty years before his inauguration, 47 per cent of the graduates were ministers, but during his 'reign' the percentage dropped to 23. Witherspoon himself was the only clergyman to sign the Declaration of Independence. He served in the Continental Congress. Moreover, as has often been pointed out, his graduates included 13 college presidents, 6 delegates to the Continental Congress, 20 senators, 24 representatives, 13 governors, 3 judges of the Supreme Court, 1 vice-president (Aaron Burr) and 1 president (James Madison). It produced also perhaps America's only true poet of the Revolution, Philip Freneau. It was to be Woodrow Wilson, Witherspoon's most eminent successor in the headship of the college, who was to sum up its character under his great forerunner: it was, he said, 'a seminary of statesmen'.[1]

Once Princeton was established, a host of schools sprang up to prepare students for it. And it was itself a progenitor. Its offspring include Washington College, in Maryland (1782), Hampden-Sidney College, in Virginia (1783), the University of Georgia (1785), the University of North Carolina (1789), Washington (1806) and Jefferson (1802) Colleges, situated only seven miles apart in western Pennsylvania, on the site of 'log schools' dating back to the 1780s, and united as Washington and Jefferson in 1865, and, in what is now Tennessee, Davidson Academy (1785), which eventually grew into the University of Nashville, Tusculum College, at Greeneville (1794), Blount College (1794), which finally became the University of Tennessee, and Newark College, the germ of the University of Delaware, which traces its descent from Alison's little school of 1743.

This is not, of course, to argue that this log-college culture, however graceful its pinnacle of Old Nassau, was the first in American educational history. As everyone knows, Harvard was founded as a Congregational College in 1636, as a result of John Harvard's legacy. Again, had plans worked out for Henrico University and College, Virginia would have been first—but the Indian massacre of 1622 ended its dream. Near the end of the century, in 1693, the Anglican College of William and Mary was established in Virginia, and in 1701, a few years later, Connecticut legislation provided for the establishment of Yale University. But the most noteworthy feature of America's educational history was the growth of a tax-supported public-school system, free to all. To New England goes much of the credit for this contribution. There the settlers acted together as a single public body, bringing to bear upon the school the concentrated resources of the community. In 1647, Massachusetts Bay legislation—followed shortly by all the New England colonies except Rhode Island—provided for

[1] T. J. Wertenbaker, op. cit.

V. L. Collins, *President Witherspoon* (Philadelphia, 1925).

L. H. Butterfield, *President Witherspoon Comes to America* (Princeton, 1953).

M. C. Tyler, 'President Witherspoon in the American Revolution', *American Hist. Review*, I (1896).

F. L. Broderick, 'The Curriculum of the College of New Jersey 1746–94', *William and Mary Quarterly*, 3rd ser. VI (1949).

D. R. Come, 'The Influence of Princeton on Higher Education in the South before 1835', ibid, II (1945).

compulsory elementary education. This was, of course, largely theory and the purpose was restricted, to train students for the ministry. The curriculum was heavily classical. Its character has been described by its own distinguished historian, S. E. Morison:

> All students, whether or not candidates for the pulpit, took a prescribed course in six of the traditional Seven Arts (Grammar, Logic, Rhetoric, Arithmetic, Geometry and Astronomy), in the Three Philosophies (Metaphysics, Ethics and Natural Science), and in Greek, Hebrew and Ancient History. Latin was supposed to have been mastered in grammar school; it was the language of instruction, and of most of the textbooks. It was a very similar programme to that which many founders of New England had studied at Old Cambridge, containing the same three elements: the medieval arts and philosophies, founded largely on the works of Aristotle; the more serious Renaissance study of Greek and Hebrew; and the lighter Renaissance study of classical belles-lettres. All these subjects were considered essential to a gentleman's education. The professional study of theology began only after taking the bachelor's degree. Undergraduates were given only as much divinity as was supposed to be requisite for an educated Christian layman; and that, of course, was a great deal according to our standards. It included the careful study and analysis of the Bible in the original tongues, a short handbook of Protestant divinity (Ames's *Medulla* or Wolleb's *Abridgement of Christian Divinity*), taking notes on two long sermons every Lord's Day, and being quizzed on them subsequently.
>
> The bachelor's course was intended to be, and was, a liberal education for the times, having no practical or professional value, equally suitable for a future divine, physician or ruler. President Oakes addressed one of his graduating classes as 'gentlemen, educated like gentlemen'. It was intended to introduce young men to the best thought and literature of past ages, not to make them receptive to the thought of their own time.

Most of the professors were, of course, clergymen. The entrance age was low, the subjects fixed and limited. Even in Congregational New England there are clearly parallels here with the Scottish universities, and differences between them and those of England—the preference for a location in or near the chief town of a province or region, the tendency to confuse or identify 'college' and 'university', the fairly well realised aim of 'the open door' in favour of poor boys of talent, the serious and studious tone of life, and some elements of democracy in the academic community. To men bred in the Scottish mode, therefore, the American colleges must have seemed familiar in spirit, aims and needs.[1]

Harvard's total staff throughout the eighteenth century was a president, a professor of mathematics and four tutors, and by the Revolution its enrolment was about 180; Yale had 170 and Princeton 100. Franklin's father wisely decided not to put him in for Harvard, partly because it was too expensive, partly because of 'the mean living many so educated were afterwards able to obtain'. And Franklin's Silence Dogood has little that is kind to say about it. Her contemporary portrait is a little franker than S. E. Morison's:

> Riches and Poverty kept the gate, and Poverty rejected those whom Riches did not recommend. Within the temple Learning sat on a high throne reached by difficult steps. Most of the worshippers 'contented themselves to sit at the foot with Madam Idleness and her maid Ignorance'. . . . 'Every beetle-skull seemed well satisfied with his own portion of learning, though perhaps he was e'en just as ignorant as ever.' Once out of the temple, 'some I perceived took to merchandising, others to travelling, some to one thing, some to another, and some to nothing; and many of them from henceforth, for want of patrimony, lived as poor as church mice, being unable to dig and ashamed to beg, and to live by their wits it was impossible . . . I reflected in my mind on the extreme folly of those parents who, blind to their children's dullness and insensible of the solidity of their skulls, because they think their purses can afford it will needs send them to the Temple of Learning, where, for want of a suitable genius, they learn little more than how to carry themselves handsomely and enter a room genteelly (which might as well be acquired at a dancing-school), and from whence they return, after abundance of trouble and charge, as great blockheads as ever, only more proud and self-conceited.'

Perhaps Franklin was put off by the recollections of the career of Nathaniel Eaton, Harvard's first head, who was called 'professor', not 'president'. He was recommended for his knowledge of theology but he starved his students, whipped his assistants, embezzled the funds and wisely fled to Virginia where, according to John Winthrop, he 'succumbed to vice, being usually drunken, as the custom is there'. Or perhaps he was put off, as was young

[1] S. E. Morison, *The Founding of Harvard College* (Cambridge, 1935) and *Harvard College in the Seventeenth Century* (2 vols., Cambridge, 1936).

John Adams, by the fact that the students were listed by social class, not by merit, 'from the brave coat, lace embroidered to the gray coat shading down'. Harvard, like the Ritz, was open to all.[1]

In the South, the farms and plantations were so widely separated that community schools like those in the more compact settlements were impossible. Perhaps some still agreed with Governor Berkeley, 'Thank God there are no schools and no printing presses in Virginia, and I hope there will be none for these 100 years.' Planters sometimes joined with their nearest neighbours and hired tutors to teach all the children within reach. The children of wealthy planters were sent to England for schooling, but this ceased in 1776 as, with the end of entail, it became impossible to afford it. 'But why send an American youth to England for education?': so Jefferson rationalised the consequences of his philosophy. 'If he goes to England he learns drinking, horse-racing and boxing. These are the peculiarities of English education.' In the more thickly settled areas, a few neighbourhood schools provided instruction but, in general, the individual planter was obliged to assume the cost and responsibility of hiring tutors. Many of these were Scots, and one, John Warden, used this ladder to become a Virginian and later a distinguished figure at the Virginia Bar. But these were not uniformly popular. It was feared that they would teach the children the Scotch dialect 'which they can never wear off'. Young Philip Fithian, having graduated from Princeton, served as a tutor in 1773 to the children of Robert Carter of Nomini Hall in Virginia. And Carter was frank with him.

> He informed me that he does indeed prefer a tutor for his children who has been educated upon the Continent, not on a supposition that such are better scholars, or that they are of better principles, or of more agreeable tempers; but only on account of pronunciation in the English Language, (as most of his children are to be

[1] S. E. Morison, op. cit.
Clifford K. Shipton, *Biographical Sketches of Those Who Attended Harvard College* (*Sibley's Harvard Graduates*, Cambridge and Boston, 1933–62).
L. W. Labaree *et al.* (eds.), *The Papers of Benjamin Franklin*, Vol. I (Yale, 1959).
Robert F. Seybolt, *The Public Schools of Colonial Boston* (Cambridge, 1935).
— *The Public Schoolmasters of Colonial Boston* (Cambridge, 1939).

taught chiefly in this) in which he allows young gentlemen educated in good schools on the Continent, to excel the Scotch young gentlemen, & indeed most of the English.

And he discovered franker sentiments from visitors to Nomini Hall.

> Mr *Lee* in our room raved against the Scotch—He swore that if his sister should marry a Scotchman, he would never speak with her again; & that if he ever shall have a daughter, if she marries a Scotchman he shoots her dead at once![1]

But whatever this distaste by the 1770s, there can be no denial that William and Mary itself was Scotsman James Blair's achievement. Blair was an Anglican clergyman, a student at Marischal College, Aberdeen, and a graduate of Edinburgh, whom the Bishop of London sent over as his Commissary and who for over half a century remained the head of the established Church in Virginia and a powerful figure in Virginia politics. He it was who instituted far-reaching reforms in the clergy, securing for them better salaries, filling vacant parishes with men of piety and ability, and insisting upon a better observance of the liturgy. When he returned to the colony after securing a charter for the College and a grant of money from the Crown—£2,000 sterling, plus 20,000 acres of land plus the revenue of 1d. per lb. on Virginia's and Maryland's tobacco exports—he brought with him plans for the main building drawn by Sir Christopher Wren. Blair himself was president of the college for many years. Its subjects were Languages, Divinity and Natural Philosophy. It is said that when he brought an order to the Lord of the Exchequer for the £2,000 which the King and Queen had granted to the college, the latter demurred strongly. 'But, my Lord', said Blair, 'the college is designed to educate young men for the ministry, and we in Virginia have souls to be saved as well as you in England.' 'Damn your souls', was the reply, 'make tobacco.'

Blair made himself a power in the colony, chiefly through the

---

[1] H. D. Farish (ed.), *The Present State of Virginia, and the College*, by Henry Hartwell, James Blair and Edward Chilton (Williamsburg, 1940).

— *The Journal and Letters of Philip Vickers Fithian 1773-4* (Williamsburg, 1945).

L. B. Wright, *The First Gentlemen of Virginia* (Boston, 1940).

— 'The "Gentlemen's Library" in Early Virginia', *Huntington Library Quarterly*, I (1937).

W. G. McCabe, 'The First University in America', *Virginia Magazine of History and Biography*, XXX (1922).

influence of the great English prelates. He quarrelled with three successive governors and his power was such that it was they who were removed, not him. The planter aristocracy were inclined to snub him as an upstart, but they did so at their peril, for he won victory after victory over them. In the end, after he had married a Virginia lady of good family, Sarah Harrison, the First Families of Virginia took him to their hearts. He failed to reform the Church. Perhaps in the end he had ceased to want to. He died aged 87 and as William Gooch wrote, he left £10,000 to the great comfort of his nephew, his heir.

> A rupture he has had above 40 years concealed from everybody but one friend, mortified and killed him. If his belly had been as sound as his head and breast, he might have lived many years longer.[1]

There can, I think, be no question that the most enterprising of the colonies in the educational sphere was Pennsylvania for Quaker as well as Scottish reasons. The first school, begun in 1683, taught reading, writing and the keeping of accounts. Thereafter, in some fashion, every Quaker community provided for the elementary teaching of its children. More advanced training—in classical languages, history, literature—was offered at the Friends Public School, which still exists in Philadelphia as the William Penn Charter School. The school was free to the poor, but parents who could were required to pay tuition for their children. In Philadelphia numerous private schools with no religious affiliation taught languages, mathematics and natural science, and there were night schools for adults. Nor, in contrast with all other colonies was the education of women entirely overlooked, for private teachers instructed the daughters of prosperous Philadelphians in French, music, dancing, painting, singing, grammar, and sometimes even bookkeeping.

The advanced intellectual and cultural development of Pennsylvania reflected, in large measure, the vigorous personalities of

[1] D. E. Motley, *Life of Commissary James Blair* (Baltimore, 1901).
  Bishop W. S. Perry, *History of the American Protestant Episcopal Church (1587-1883)* (New York, 1885).
  H. B. Adams, *The College of William and Mary* (Washington, D.C., 1887).

four men, and owed much to Scotland. One of these was James Logan, a Scotch-Irish Quaker, secretary of the colony, at whose fine library young Benjamin Franklin found the latest scientific works. In 1745 Logan erected a building for his collection and bequeathed it and his books to the city. There is no doubt, however, that Franklin himself contributed more than any other single citizen to the stimulation of intellectual activity in Philadelphia. He was instrumental in creating institutions which made a permanent cultural contribution, not only to Philadelphia, but to all the colonies. He formed, for example, a club known as the Junto, which was the embryo of the American Philosophical Society. As a result of his endeavours, a public academy was founded which developed later into the University of Pennsylvania. It was certainly Franklin's energy and drive that gave impetus to the plan, his fame and standing in the community that ensured action, and his secular and scientific spirit that determined the emphasis laid by the college on English studies, its aim of providing a practical preparation for citizenship, and its avoidance of any sectarianism or religious discrimination. (This last provision was almost a precondition for success in view of the multiplicity of sects in Pennsylvania.) In his view the classical schools failed to meet the requirements of the new age, with its need for mechanics, for business and commercial training and its distinctly vernacular culture. Through Whitefield he had been impressed by what he had heard of the schools for Dissenters at Northampton, England, where the teaching of English was placed on equal footing with that of the classics. He may from him, too, have heard of Francis Hutcheson in Glasgow. In his Proposals of 1749 he made his case, though he recognised the extent of the existing preference for what he called ornamental rather than useful training. By 1750 £15,000 had been raised and classes began in the Academy in 1751. The Academy consisted of two departments, the English School, which was the heart of Franklin's proposals, and the Latin School, to which he had in effect consented for the increased support its presence might bring to the whole. To each of the two branches he had expected the trustees to pay 'an equal regard', but from the beginning the scales appeared to be weighted against the English School. Disregarding the social and educational needs of city and province, the trustees made the master of the Latin School, David Martin, rector of the institution, and voted him twice the salary of his English colleague; and as a result attendance at the English School declined in a single year to forty-one scholars. When Franklin returned from England in 1762, he was shocked by the condition of affairs at the Academy, and took the trustees severely to task for the partial performance of their trust. He recalled in later years how 'Parents . . . despairing of any reformation, withdrew their children, and placed them in private schools . . . and they have since flourished and increased by the scholars the Academy might have had, if it had performed its engagements.' The course of study stressed at the Academy led Benjamin Rush to rejoice in retrospect that his friend David Rittenhouse had escaped the pernicious influences of an educational system designed for fifteenth-century Europe and in no way adapted to New World circumstances.

Ironically enough, it was Franklin himself who was largely responsible for the two remarkable appointments that contributed most to this overdevelopment of the classical curriculum. Both of them were Scots. Francis Alison, Presbyterian divine and the finest classical scholar in America, took charge of the institution upon the death of David Martin in 1752, moving from New London to do so. Educated at Glasgow, he was described by Franklin as 'a Person of great ingenuity and learning, a catholic Divine, and what is more, an Honest Man'. The example of Alison's New London School had provided real encouragement for educational reformers in Philadelphia, and with his characteristic ability to select the best man, Franklin persuaded him to come to the Academy. More a scholar than an administrator, Alison refused the rectorship, but under his care the Latin School flourished, and its curriculum received the vigorous support so many of the trustees desired. The appointment a year later of the ardent and aggressive Anglican William Smith as rector finally cemented the supremacy of the classics. He more than anyone else, Franklin later charged, shifted emphasis from the English to the Latin School, which after 1755 was taken under the wing of the College of Philadelphia, and served as a feeder to it. Yet in fact Smith was as much the founder of what grew into the University of Pennsylvania as Franklin himself, and despite their later quarrels deserves as much credit as Old Dr Doubleface. It needed an academic head of scholastic distinction and administrative ability. The endeavours of the co-founders were indeed mutually complementary, since each of these men, the product of sharply contrasting education and cultural environment, to some extent supplied the deficiences of the other. One naturally leaned to English studies, the other to the classics. Their remarkable achievement lay in the provision of a curriculum ('devised for the education of the average man along the broadest lines of culture known to the times') that met the requirements of Quakers, Presbyterians and Anglicans, of merchants, lawyers and divines.

Born in 1727, William Smith attended (perhaps without graduating) at King's College, Aberdeen, from 1743 to 1747. He became a schoolmaster and before he was 24 had twice appeared in print, with a schoolmasters' memorial addressed to Parliament, urging the extension of the parish schools, and an article, in the *Scots Magazine*, on his educational theories. Endowed with ambition as well as ability, he saw an alternative noble prospect to the highway to London in the broad highway to America. He went to New York (as a tutor) early in 1751, and positively brimming over with ideas, he published a pamphlet there in October 1752, which, in the following April, he expanded into the justly renowned and widely influential work, *A General Idea of the College of Mirania*. Though intended to apply to New York, *Mirania* (apart from its general impact in the educational field) bore positive results in Philadelphia. It won the interest and approbation of Franklin, who had already turned his mind to problems connected with the reform and improvement of teaching within the city. On Franklin's invitation, Smith went to Philadelphia, where he was moved to write a poem (which can most charitably be called undistinguished) in praise of the educational rivalry of New York and Philadelphia—a 'nobler strife' than that of Athens and Sparta. Probably by arrangement with Franklin, Smith returned to Britain, where in December 1753 he took Anglican orders; and six months later he was back as a teacher at the Philadelphia academy. There followed the grant in May 1755 by the proprietors, Thomas and Richard Penn, of the 'additional charter of the College, Academy and Charity-School of Philadelphia', with Smith as first provost, a man still under thirty, and Alison as vice-provost and rector of the Academy. This post he kept until, in 1779, for politico-religious reasons, the charter was voided and a period of confused strife ensued, to be terminated by the erection of the University of Pennsylvania (1791).

In many respects Smith was a force second only to Franklin in the intellectual life of the city. He stimulated the creative and imaginative arts: he was friend, critic and guide to a group of young men, significantly calling themselves 'A Society of Gentlemen', who, about the years 1758-9, brought forth 'the first American musical production, the first American drama to be professionally performed, and the first American painting of permanent worth', and *The American Magazine and Monthly Chronicle*, the only literary periodical in America that enjoyed financial success before the Revolution. He raised no less than £1,000 for the College when he visited Britain ten years later. But in all his zeal and energy he was arrogant, ill-tempered when opposed, something of an intriguer. John Adams, no kind diarist about anybody, described him as 'soft, polite, insinuating, adulating, sensible, learned, industrious, indefatigable; he has art enough, and refinement upon art, to make impressions'. From the day of his appointment he intrigued, openly and in secret, to bring the College completely under Anglican control. As a result, he found it impossible to keep out of local politics. As early as 1756 his patron Benjamin Franklin wrote in exasperation to Whitefield that he wished Smith would 'learn to mind Party-writing and Party-Politicks less, and his proper Business more'. He became an open supporter of the Proprietary party and he and Franklin soon ceased to be on speaking terms.

There were signs, then, of cultural as well as a political ferment at work in Pennsylvania, especially in Franklin's Philadelphia. It was evident in the group in the next generation that gathered around Rittenhouse, the Peales and the Bartrams, of whom Franklin, and later Jefferson, were the leading spirits. Charles Brockden Brown of Philadelphia appeared as the first professional novelist and man of letters in the country, publishing *Wieland* in 1798, and following this in rapid succession with *Ormand*, *Edgar Huntley*, *Arthur Mervyn*, *Jane Talbot* and *Clara Howard*, all works of a Gothic and grotesque character. In journalism, a field in which the Scotch-Irish were later to excel, John Dunlap founded *The Pennsylvania Packet or General Advertiser* in 1771, a journal which appeared in 1784 as the first daily newspaper in the United States under the name of *The Pennsylvania Packet and General Advertiser*. Another eminent Scotch-Irishman of this era was David Ramsay, a native of Lancaster County, Pennsylvania, who later removed to South Carolina. Ramsay was the author of a *History of South Carolina, History of the Revolution in South Carolina, History of the American Revolution* and *Life of Washington*, winning fame as one of the most distinguished historians of his time.[1]

One other aspect of Scottish influence must be mentioned: the Edinburgh Medical School. Here again, indirectly, Franklin was the link. In 1761 he visited Scotland and the first outgrowth of his Scottish tour was the advent of the brilliant succession of American medical students who went to Edinburgh University, largely at his suggestion. In the spring of 1760 there arrived in London a young probationer from Philadelphia, John Morgan, destined to be the founder of the medical school of the University of Pennsylvania. Morgan seems to have been undecided whether to pursue his studies at the University of Leyden or that of Edinburgh. Leyden, where taught Boerhaave, the Nestor of the surgical profession, had hitherto attracted a great number of English and American pupils. Franklin, however, in the enthusiasm engendered by his recent visit, persuaded Morgan to matriculate at Edinburgh. This was a pregnant decision, since the coterie of Pennsylvania neophytes who came over in the next decade followed Morgan's example, and Edinburgh became the academic Mecca for transatlantic medical students just as the Middle Temple in London already was for practitioners of the law.

From 1749, when John Moultrie, of South Carolina, was made a doctor of medicine of the University of Edinburgh, to the close of the century, no fewer than 117 Americans received the medical

[1] F. B. Tolles, *James Logan and the Culture of Provincial America* (Boston, 1957).

F. N. Thorpe, *Benjamin Franklin and the University of Pennsylvania* (New York, 1892).

L. W. La baree *et al.* (eds.), *The Papers of Benjamin Franklin* (Yale, 1959), *passim.*

H. W. Smith, *Life and Correspondence of William Smith* (Philadelphia, 1879–80).

W. Smith, *Account of the College, Academy and Charitable School of Philadelphia in Pennsylvania* (ed. Adams, with commentary by T. Woody, 1951).

A. F. Gegenheimer, *William Smith, Educator and Churchman 1727–1803* (New York, 1943).

G. W. Corner (ed.), *The Autobiography of Benjamin Rush* (American Philosophical Society, 1948).

L. H. Butterfield (ed.), *The Letters of Benjamin Rush* (American Philosophical Society, 2 vols., 1951).

E. D. Owen, 'Where did Benjamin Franklin get the idea for his Academy?', *Pennsylvania Magazine of History and Biography*, Vol. 58 (1932).

degree of that institution alone; while uncounted others, like Thomas Parke, Samuel Powel Griffitts and Benjamin Smith Barton, studied there. By the 1780s nearly five hundred students of medicine were in the city—John R. B. Rodgers in the spring of 1785 said that Dr Monro had 399 in his anatomy class alone— and of this number there were always fifteen or twenty Americans, usually two or three of them from Philadelphia.

But, despite the merits of Edinburgh and the affection in which it was held, it did not stand the test of 1776. At the beginning of the American Revolution, all the Scottish graduates in America, except Dr Bard of New York who remained true to the Crown, enlisted in the patriot army. Yet a singular destiny attended their military careers. Potts, broken in spirit and body by his unappreciated services with the Northern Army at Ticonderoga, came back to a premature death in Reading. Rush resigned his commission in 1778 after a series of quarrels with his departmental chiefs —the evidence of a pride in his own talents that was to mark his long career. Shippen was court-martialled for alleged irregularities in his military hospital. Morgan was displaced through the intrigues of an ignoble cabal in the Congress. Perhaps the aggrieved professors at the Edinburgh Medical School saw in these calamities the visitation of a Calvinistic deity outraged at the traitorous misapplication to Revolutionary purposes of knowledge obtained in a good Scotch college. But as Bismarck later put it, God was in the end to be on the side of fools, drunkards and the U.S.A.[1]

It is an impossible task within an hour to trace the impact of one people or perhaps of three groups of peoples on another country. Clearly the main impact of Scots and Ulster Scots was on the Middle Colonies and the South—New England stayed separate,

[1] J. Bennett Nolan, *Benjamin Franklin in Scotland and Ireland* (Philadelphia, 1938).

Nathan Goodman, *Benjamin Rush, Physician and Citizen 1746–1813* (Philadelphia, 1934).

Frances R. Packard, *History of Medicine in the United States*, 2 vols. (New York, 1931).

William Pepper, 'The Medical Side of Benjamin Franklin', *University of Pennsylvania Medical Bulletin*, XXIII (1910).

Whitfield J. Bell, Jnr., 'Philadelphia Medical Students in Europe 1750–1800', *The Pennsylvania Mag. of Hist. and Biog.*, Vol. 67 (1943).

a Congregational countryside. Reduced to individuals this could have been the story of Commissary Blair in Virginia, of William Smith in Pennsylvania and of John Witherspoon in New Jersey —two of them, be it noted, Anglicans, and two of them, the same two, being Aberdonians. Or the story could be told as the story of Princeton and of Princeton men. Or it could be told as a story of American Colonial medicine, an overseas colony of the Edinburgh Medical School. Yet all such telling omits or minimises one fundamental fact: the role of Glasgow and the role of Revolutionary ideas. Obviously these were carried quite readily by Presbyterians. The British Army in the Revolution burned Presbyterian churches as 'sedition-shops' and consigned to the flames, as texts of rebellion, all Bibles with Scottish versions of the psalms. But Witherspoon had no monopoly of these ideas and there were many other Founding Fathers.

One of these was Benjamin Franklin. Franklin was not, of course, a Scot, and indeed took pride in being, to about 1770 or even later, an Old England Man. Handled right, he need never have been a rebel. But by 1774 he was. And if there was one decisive influence on him in Britain it was the liberal dissenting critical spirit of his Scottish friends—royal physician Sir John Pringle, Lord Kames, Adam Smith, David Hume, Principal Robertson and his friend and printer William Strahan, whom he called 'Straney'. If some of these men were themselves, of course, largely Tories, the climate of opinion in which they moved was critical, dissenting and challenging. Hume was pro-American; Kames had much sympathy; Smith favoured free trade and an experiment in federalism; Boswell even differed from Johnson on America. 'Orthodox' or 'Evangelical' Church opinion was pro-American—the Reverend Charles Nisbet of Montrose followed his friend Witherspoon to America in 1785, to become president of Dickinson College. Every one of the American doctors trained in the Edinburgh Medical School before 1776—except one, Dr Bard of New York—became, as I have said, a Revolutionary, and most of them were in Washington's army. Political Scotland, the Scotland of Bute, Dundas and Lord Adam Gordon, was solidly Tory. Most of its Edinburgh and Aberdeen academics, aware of the need for butter on their bread, were the same, including Principal Robertson. (One has to say Edinburgh and Aberdeen because the Glasgow of John Millar and John Anderson had its conspicuous

Radicals.) But the mood among the students they produced was Radical and dissenting, and for this one other name must be mentioned, Frances Hutcheson. Glasgow thus comes belatedly into the list, and for other reasons than tobacco.

This is a subject that still needs clarification. Hutcheson's formal philosophy has been described often enough, as have his contributions to classical economic theory. His politics have been largely ignored, though Professor Caroline Robbins of Bryn Mawr contributed a most interesting paper on him to the *William & Mary Quarterly* in 1954. He had a host of friends and followers in America, as in Scotland. He was propounding in Glasgow a theory of the right of resistance to tyranny forty years before 1776. His works appear in Smith's plans for the College of Philadelphia and Frances Alison was dictating to students passages from him in 1759 and 1760. His writings became set books at Yale.

He was born in Armagh, son and grandson of Presbyterian ministers, educated at Glasgow University and professor there for sixteen years. He was greatly influenced by the Irish liberal, Robert Molesworth, who wanted an educational system run by philosophers, not clerics, in which English and History, Economics and Politics would be the main subjects of study. He believed in Federalism, even in Britain in 1689; he believed in the right of resistance. He went even further—to the idea of Colonial independence, religious liberty, the happiness of the greatest number and the welfare state. He wrote in a Scottish context, but what he said was highly relevant to colonists ripe to revolt. And he lectured not in Latin but in English—a point Franklin noted, and which his own university copied.

The Revolution was the product of many forces, but insufficient attention has been paid to such dissenting and levelling ideas. Bernard Bailyn of Harvard has recently and brilliantly demonstrated the need to look at these forces afresh in his essay 'The Transforming Radicalism of the American Revolution' that prefaces the first volume of his series *Pamphlets of the American Revolution*. These forces included, of course, the influences of Locke and Milton, Sidney and Harrington, which so greatly influenced Hutcheson (the Glasgow student debating society was called *Oceana*). They included the sermons of Bishop Hoadly. They included the sermons of Francis Makemie, whom Lord Cornbury, the Governor of New York, had sent to gaol not merely because he preached without a licence but because he was a 'Jack-of-all trades . . . and a disturber of governments'. Presbyterianism in religion meant democracy in politics, government by 'covenant and compact' in State as in Church. And among such influences we must add the name of Thomas Gordon, that little-known Aberdonian who joined forces with John Trenchard, the West Country squire, to produce the weekly *Independent Whig* and *Cato's Letters*. Their writings, which circulated in the Colonies and were frequently quoted, were as important as those of Locke as a statement of the nature of political liberty. Harrington's ideas reached Jefferson by way of his own beloved teacher, William Small, of Aberdeen. And Witherspoon at Princeton spread the social contract views in language strikingly like that of Jefferson:

> if they (the laws) are found to be pernicious and destructive of the ends of the union, they (the people) may certainly break up the society, recall their obligation, and resettle the whole upon a better footing . . . But this is only when it becomes manifestly more advantageous to unsettle the government altogether, than to submit to tyranny.

Another force making for criticism was the influential non-conformist political lobby, the Protestant Dissenting Deputies. And the fact that this American radicalism often got recognition in Scotland gave it further stimulus. When Jonathan Mayhew's *Discourse Concerning Unlimited Submission*—the most famous sermon preached in pre-Revolutionary America—reached Britain, it won the approval of no less a person than the renowned latitudinarian Bishop of Winchester, Benjamin Hoadly. And Avery, Chairman of the Dissenting Deputies, got for Mayhew an honorary doctorate from Aberdeen. It was a great honour, and one he appreciated. It speaks much for Mayhew's spirit, however, that much as he appreciated the honour, he resented the condescension implied in the surprise expressed at the fact that such a book should come out of a remote province.

It was in this province, however, that by 1776 Radicalism was to triumph. It was this group, the Protestants of Scotland, of Ireland and of North America, who produced the literary manifestos of discontent. The colony that rebelled had the support of John Anderson, of John Millar and of John Millar's pupil, Thomas Muir, and of Frances Hutcheson's pupil, Joseph Priestley. They were only a handful, but they believed that America was fighting not for the rights of Americans only but also for the rights of Scotsmen, and for those of all mankind. Scotland made its distinct contribution to American independence. And America had its own contribution to make to Scotland over the next two centuries in helping to keep alive a sense of the distinctness of the Scot —overseas as well as at home.[1]

[1] Caroline Robbins, *The Eighteenth-Century Commonwealthman* (Cambridge, 1961).

B. Bailyn (ed.), *Pamphlets of the American Revolution*, Vol. I (Harvard, 1965), especially Introductory Essay, 'The Transforming Radicalism of the American Revolution'.

Bishop Perry, op. cit.

H. L. Ganter, 'William Small, Jefferson's Beloved Teacher', *William and Mary Quarterly*, 3rd ser. (1945–), Vol. 2.

J. Clive and B. Bailyn, 'England's Cultural Provinces: Scotland and America', *William and Mary Quarterly*, 3rd ser., Vol. XI (1954).

P. J. Anderson, 'Aberdeen Influence on American Universities', *Aberdeen University Review*, Vol. V (1917–18).

O. Handlin, 'James Burgh', *Proceedings of the Massachusetts Historical Society*, Vol. 73 (1961).

N. Hans, 'Franklin, Jefferson and the English Radicals at the end of the eighteenth century', *Proceedings of American Philosophical Society*, Vol. 98 (1954).

CHAPTER III

Ulster Emigration, 1783–1815

by Maldwyn A. Jones

Few ethnic groups in the United States have been more written about than the Scotch-Irish. Ever since George Chambers's pioneer study appeared in 1856[1] there has been a steady stream of books and articles dealing with the place of the Scotch-Irish in American history. Perhaps the most productive period of Scotch-Irish historiography was the last decade of the nineteenth century, when an army of devoted amateur scholars of Scotch-Irish descent set themselves the task of commemorating the achievements of their forbears. These enthusiasts were, perhaps, somewhat uncritical in their approach but they produced many painstaking studies which are still of value to scholars.[2] In this way the foundations were laid for the more comprehensive works of Charles A. Hanna, C. K. Bolton and Henry J. Ford which appeared early in the present century.[3] Such works still tended, it is true, to be pietistic in tone, and it is only very recently that the subject has been tackled in a spirit of scholarly objectivity. Thanks, however, to the work of scholars like Wayland F. Dunaway, James G. Leyburn and R. J. Dickson the study of Scotch-Irish emigration has now

[1] George Chambers, *A Tribute to the Principles, Virtues, Habits and Public Usefulness of the Irish and Scotch Early Settlers of Pennsylvania* (Chambersburg, Pa., 1856).
[2] For typical examples of their work see Scotch-Irish Society of America, *Proceedings and Addresses*, 10 vols. (Nashville, Tenn., 1890–1900).
[3] Charles A. Hanna, *The Scotch-Irish, or the Scot in North Britain, North Ireland and North America*, 2 vols. (New York and London, 1902); C. K. Bolton, *Scotch-Irish Pioneers in Ulster and America* (Boston, 1910); Henry Jones Ford, *The Scotch-Irish in America* (Princeton, 1915).

46

reached maturity.[1] No longer are we given a mere catalogue of the achievements in politics and war of a few exceptional, and therefore unrepresentative, individuals. Emphasis has instead come to be placed on the social and economic implications of the movement and on the fate of the anonymous masses who composed it. And in the writing of a more sophisticated history of the Scotch-Irish a good deal of legend has been swept away.

Nevertheless the story of Scotch-Irish emigration has been told only in part. Practically everything that has been written on the subject has been concerned with the period up to and including the American Revolution. The pre-1776 Ulster background, the part played by the Scotch-Irish in settling the colonies, the contributions they made to the guarding of the frontier, to the establishment of Presbyterianism in the New World and to the winning of American independence—these have been perennial themes. What part, if any, the Scotch-Irish played in peopling the United States after 1783 is a question which historians, amateur and professional alike, have chosen to ignore.

This preoccupation with the colonial period is not difficult to explain. It has owed something to the fact that, until fairly recently, historians generally were in the habit of looking at the past in narrowly political terms. Not unnaturally, those who wrote about the Scotch-Irish shared the prevailing point of view. To them 1776 seemed as logical a terminus in the history of immigration as it was in American political and constitutional history. And although in recent decades historical study has become less exclusively political in emphasis, traditional forms of synthesis and of periodisation have persisted.

But a more important reason for terminating the Scotch-Irish story with the American Revolution arose from the circumstances in which many of the works on the subject were written. The closing decade of the nineteenth century was a period in which the place of the immigrant in American society was under critical scrutiny.[2] The unprecedented flood of immigrants then pouring

[1] Wayland F. Dunaway, *The Scotch-Irish of Colonial Pennsylvania* (Chapel Hill, North Carolina, 1944); James G. Leyburn, *The Scotch-Irish: A Social History* (Chapel Hill, North Carolina, 1962); R. J. Dickson, *Ulster Emigration to Colonial America, 1718–1775* (London, 1966).
[2] See John Higham, *Strangers in the Land: Patterns of American Nativism, 1860–1925* (New Brunswick, New Jersey, 1955) and Barbara M. Solomon, *Ancestors and Immigrants: A Changing New England Tradition* (Cambridge, Mass., 1956).

into the United States had aroused the hostility of many native-born Americans and had produced a growing demand for restriction. Lending strength to the restrictionists was a developing race-consciousness which stressed the 'Anglo-Saxon' character of American culture and which drew a sharp distinction between 'colonists' who had arrived in America before 1776 and 'immigrants' who had come later.[1] According to this interpretation the colonists were bold, adventurous people who, mainly for idealistic reasons, had settled in a distant wilderness; to them alone belonged the credit for developing the country and for establishing its political and religious institutions. Immigrants, by contrast, were less worthy folk who had simply come to America to cash in on the material prosperity created by the efforts of earlier comers. To maintain this distinction between colonists and immigrants was the purpose of the exclusive patriotic societies founded at this time by those who prided themselves on their colonial ancestry, and so successfully did they argue their case that their point of view became generally accepted.

In a situation in which ancestry determined status it was not surprising that Scotch-Irish apologists should have been at pains to establish their colonial origins. They were doubly anxious to do so because a good deal of nativist hostility was directed against Irish Catholics. To avoid sharing in the opprobrium that befell the Irish generally the Scotch-Irish in America felt it to be necessary to demonstrate that they constituted a distinct ethnic group which was not to be confused with the 'mere' Irish, and that they had come to America as colonists rather than as part of the mass exodus from Ireland that followed the Great Famine.

This was, of course, no more than the truth. Yet the distinction between colonists and immigrants is now acknowledged to have been largely unreal. As Theodore Roosevelt once remarked, the term 'colonist' is 'a euphemistic name for an immigrant who came over in the steerage of a sailing vessel in the seventeenth century instead of in the steerage of a steamer in the nineteenth century'.[2] Certainly the distinction seems artificial if one extends one's enquiries into Ulster emigration to the post-Revolutionary

[1] See, for example, Richmond Mayo-Smith, *Emigration and Immigration* (New York, 1908), pp. 35–6.
[2] Quoted in *A Report on World Population Migrations as Related to the United States of America* (Washington, D.C., 1956), p. 47.

period. The Revolution proved in fact to be no more than a temporary interruption to emigration. The conditions which had led more than 250,000 people to leave Ulster in the half century before 1776 induced a further 100,000 or so to follow suit in the three decades after 1783, and the number would undoubtedly have been much larger but for the restrictive policy of the British Government.

It cannot be denied that the causes of emigration after 1783 were mainly economic, but this had also been the case during the colonial period.[1] As for the view that the post-1783 emigrants constituted a less self-sufficient class than the colonists, the reverse would appear to have been the case. For most of the colonial period the bulk of Ulster emigrants had been forced by their poverty to become indentured servants,[2] but those who emigrated to the newly independent United States were generally capable of paying their own way. They included, moreover, a considerable leavening of professional men and of the moderately well-to-do They also included, especially after 1790, numbers of political refugees who proved to be just as active in American politics as their colonial predecessors, while Scotch-Irish immigrants generally were no less prominent in the war of 1812 than in the struggle for American independence.

Emigration from Ulster, which had been unusually heavy in the early 1770s, came to an abrupt halt in the summer of 1775 when news was received of the firing at Lexington and Concord.[3] For the next eight years emigration was completely at a standstill, and the many vessels which sailed from Ireland for America carried not emigrants but troops and munitions of war.

But even before the war was officially over the exodus from the north of Ireland began again. The first departures for the United States took place early in August 1783—a month before the peace treaty was signed in Versailles. Before the end of the year about 5,000 emigrants had departed, roughly 1,500 of them from Belfast, 1,500 more from Londonderry and Newry, and a further 1,000 from Dublin.[4] In the following year the outpouring exceeded 10,000, perhaps a record for Irish emigration up to that time.[5]

[1] Dickson, *Ulster Emigration*, pp. 6–15.
[2] Ibid, pp. 87–97.   [3] Ibid, pp. 68–9.
[4] *Belfast News Letter*, 8 August 1783, 4 June 1784; B.M., Addl. MS 33100, p. 24, J. Hamilton to Mr Secretary Hamilton, 5 August 1783.
[5] F.O. 4/7. Phineas Bond to the Duke of Leeds, 10 Nov. 1789, enclosure no. 43.

What had made possible this revived movement was the resumption of transatlantic commerce. In the eighteenth century and, indeed, well into the nineteenth, there were no passenger vessels as such, and emigrants had to rely for passage on the merchant ships whose primary function was the conveyance of freight. There had long been a lively trade between the north of Ireland and America, with Irish linen and provisions being exchanged for American flaxseed, flour and tobacco. But after 1783, thanks to a series of enactments granting Ireland virtual free trade with the United States,[1] Ulster's American trade flourished as never before.

The pattern of the emigrant traffic immediately after 1783 was much as it had been in colonial days. The most popular emigrant port was Londonderry, though Belfast was never far behind, with Newry, Sligo, Larne and Killybegs following in that order. About twenty-five vessels were regularly employed in the emigrant trade in the 1780s and 1790s, many of them American-owned, and they carried on the average about 5,000 passengers annually.[2] Until about 1800 the great majority of emigrant ships took their passengers to the Delaware ports of Philadelphia, Newcastle and Wilmington, but New York became steadily more popular and there was always a sizeable movement to Baltimore and Charleston.

Even before 1776 the British Government had been uneasy about the continuing emigration from the north of Ireland,[3] and when the American Colonies became independent, official misgivings multiplied. At first, however, the reports received in London did not suggest that those who were leaving constituted a particularly valuable class. Thus the customs officer at Newry reported in August 1783 that three vessels had just sailed for America:[4]

From the best information that could be obtained from the passengers themselves, and from the owners of the vessels, there were not any people of real property who went; a very few people (amongst whom was an unbeneficed clergyman from this town)

[1] 20 Geo. III, cc. 6, 10 and 18.
[2] F.O. 4/7. Bond to the Duke of Leeds, 10 Nov. 1789, enclosure no. 43; F.O. 4/11. Bond to Grenville, 8 Oct. 1791, enclosure.
[3] Dickson, *Ulster Emigration*, p. 181.
[4] B.M. Addl. MS 33100, p. 24, J. Hamilton to Mr Secretary Hamilton, 5 Aug. 1783.

carried some little property in ventures. The greater part were of the lower order of tradesmen such as weavers, smiths, joiners, etc., etc., besides numbers of no occupation that went as servants. Those that had any property went with a view of settling in the country if they found any encouragement, but with no fixed plan that I can hear of. It seems probable that the great scarcity of provisions in this part of the Kingdom induced many to go, more especially as reports were industriously propagated of the great plenty and cheapness of provisions in America. The accounts from America as to the state of such goods that went first to that continent are, I am told, very discouraging, and will probably continue to damp the spirit of emigration, and the people now offering to go, I am well informed, are almost entirely of a very inferior class.

Not all observers would have agreed with this assessment. Thus the Belfast correspondent of an American newspaper claimed during that same summer that the emigrants leaving the country 'in such prodigious numbers are not the refuse of the country; . . . they are those that form the yeomanry of the land . . . who . . . take with them from £300 to £700 and the industrious, careful linen weaver, who has scraped together a sufficiency to transport himself and family'.[1] Then in 1784 it was reported from Sligo that the brig *Rose* had sailed for Philadelphia with more than 200 passengers, 'most of whom were persons of distinction, and some of our best artisans with their families'.[2]

Because of the contradictory nature of the evidence it is impossible to speak with certainty of the groups making up emigration at this time. What one can be sure of is that events did not bear out the optimistic prediction of the Newry customs officer that the movement would soon decline. It continued in fact on such an extensive scale that by 1788 the Government felt moved to demand reports on the subject from its consuls in the United States. It was anxious for some indication of the number of departures and it wanted particularly to learn whether the emigrants consisted of indentured servants or fare-paying passengers and what inducements, if any, were being held out to them to leave.

[1] Quoted in R. Fenton Duvall, *Philadelphia's Maritime Commerce with the British Empire, 1783–1789* (unpublished Ph. D. thesis, University of Pennsylvania, 1960), p. 458.
[2] *B.N.L.*, 11 June 1784.

The replies received in London were extremely revealing. They disclosed, firstly, that immigration to the United States was predominantly Scotch-Irish. Thus Phineas Bond, the consul at Philadelphia reported that, of the 26,364 immigrants who had arrived in the ports of the Delaware in the seven years 1783–9, only 1,893 had been German and all the rest had been 'Scotch and Irish, but chiefly Irish' from Ulster ports.[1] Secondly the consuls were agreed that most emigrants did not now travel as indentured servants, as had been the case earlier; they came instead as fare-paying passengers. Bond reported in November 1789 that 'few redemptioners or servants have recently arrived from Ireland, the passengers from thence have been chiefly such as have paid their passage money before they embarked'.[2] Similar remarks were made by Consul George Millar about the recent arrivals from Belfast and Larne at Charleston,[3] and in 1791 Sir John Temple, the Consul-General at New York, expressed the opinion that the immigrants from the north of Ireland 'would be a very great loss to that part of His Majesty's Dominions for they are not servants or redemptioners, but people who paid their passage before they embarked, and immediately on their arrival here went back into the country, well-clad and with money in their pockets . . .'.[4]

The decline of the servant trade, to which these reports testified, had in fact begun even before the Revolution. Thus the *Belfast News Letter* could remark as early as 1773 that whereas in the past it had been 'chiefly the very meanest of the People that went off, mostly in the Station of Indented Servants', most of those now going were 'people employed in the Linen Manufacture, or Farmers, and of some Property'.[5] The great majority, moreover, had paid their own passage which amounted, incidentally, to £3.10s. per head. Then from 1783 onwards the proportion of servants declined very rapidly until, in the course of the 1790s, there were none at all. This conclusion is borne out not only by the consular reports but by the changing emphasis of the shipping advertisements in Ulster newspapers. In 1783 such advertisements, though already addressed primarily to fare-paying passengers, usually contained a reference to the captain's willingness to take

[1] F.O. 4/7. Bond to the Duke of Leeds, 10 Nov. 1789, enclosure no. 43.
[2] Ibid.
[3] F.O. 4/8. Millar to the Duke of Leeds, 28 Jan. 1790.
[4] F.O. 4/11. Temple to Grenville, 5 Oct. 1791.
[5] B.N.L., 6 Apl. 1773; see also the discussion in Dickson, *Ulster Emigration*, pp. 95–7.

'a few indented servants'.[1] Ten years later, however, references of this kind had entirely disappeared. Shipping advertisements addressed to emigrants were now concerned solely with the excellent sailing qualities of the vessels, the roominess of the passenger accommodation, the reasonableness of the fares, and the experience and considerateness of the captains.

Just why the Ulster servant trade should have come to an end at this time is not easy to say. But it was certainly not the result of any falling off in the American demand for bound labour. Despite the humanitarianism of the Revolution few Americans were yet disposed to question whether such an institution was compatible with the principles of the Declaration of Independence.[2] Redemptioners and indentured servants from Germany continued to be imported into the United States for nearly forty years after the Revolution, and as late as 1819 they were being eagerly sought after by American purchasers.[3]

A more likely explanation lies in the disinclination of ships' captains to engage in the servant trade now that fare-paying passengers were forthcoming in sufficient numbers to fill their ships. The conveyance of servants had always been a precarious and troublesome business. Though considerable profits could sometimes be made, there was always the risk that an outbreak of disease during the voyage or a sudden decline in the demand for labour could scale down the value of the cargo.[4] Moreover, servants could create serious disciplinary problems during the voyage. For example, during the voyage of the ship *Liberty* from Belfast to Philadelphia in 1783, a mutiny had broken out among the indentured men servants. The *Belfast News Letter* reported:[5]

Not contented with the best usage, plenty of good provisions and a daily portion of grog, [they] insisted on having access to the

[1] See, for example, advertisements for ship *Richard and Thomas*, B.N.L., 18 May 1784, and for the ship *George*, B.N.L., 22 Feb. 1785.
[2] William Miller, 'The Effects of the American Revolution on Indentured Servitude' *Pennsylvania History*, Vol. VII, no. 3 (July 1940), pp. 131–41.
[3] Cheesman A. Herrick, *White Servitude in Pennsylvania* (Philadelphia, 1926), pp. 264–7; Eugene I. McCormac, *White Servitude in Maryland, 1634–1820* (Baltimore, 1904), pp. 109–10.
[4] Abbot E. Smith, *Colonists in Bondage: White Servitude and Convict Labor in America, 1607–1776* (Chapel Hill, 1947), p. 39.
[5] B.N.L., 28 Oct. 1783.

women, which being refused them, they broke in the bulk head that separated the females from them. A mutinous riot ensued in which, before the insurgents could be properly secured, one of them [had] paid his life forfeit to his temerity.

Still another difficulty was that there were long delays at the port of arrival while the servants were being sold off, and not infrequently servants absconded before purchasers had been found for them. And if, for all these reasons, ship captains had become less enthusiastic than before about recruiting servants, the publicity given in 1788 to cases in which Ulster servants had been ill-used may well have reduced the numbers of those willing to sign indentures.[1]

The final blow, however, was the decision of the Government to place new restrictions on the emigration of skilled workmen who had long constituted the most sought-after class of servants. Official disquiet at the rising volume of emigration from Ireland became steadily more marked after 1783. There were fears that, if the movement were not checked, the northern counties of Ireland would be depopulated, with a consequent weakening of the Protestant interest.[2] But concern centred even more around the fact that a large proportion of the emigrants possessed skills which could at no distant date make the United States an industrial competitor of Great Britain. Fears of a loss of skilled labour had led the British Government, from 1718 onwards, to forbid artisans in certain specified industries from departing out of the King's Dominions, and now in 1783 a new measure made it an offence to attempt to 'contract with, entice, persuade, solicit or seduce any manufacturer, workman or artificer' to emigrate.[3] This was the Act under which one Thomas Philpot was prosecuted in Dublin in 1788. In the first prosecution of its kind, he was found guilty of endeavouring to entice skilled workmen to leave Ireland for America as servants, and was fined £500 and imprisoned for one year.[4]

The Act of 1783 was supplemented in 1795 by a Proclamation of the Lord Lieutenant of Ireland forbidding masters of emigrant ships to afford passage to artificers or manufacturers, and requir-

[1] Ibid, 15, 18, 25 Apl. 1788.
[2] *Annual Report of the American Historical Association*, 1897, pp. 491–3. Bond to Grenville, 8 Oct. 1791.
[3] 23 Geo. III, c. 14.
[4] *B.N.L.*, 30 May 1788.

ing them to hand to the customs officers before sailing sworn statements giving the names and occupations of all persons on board.[1] Yet this measure did nothing to check the growing number of departures from Ulster. The difficulties of enforcing it were described in April 1796 in a letter to London from the Collector at Derry. The trouble was, he declared, that in Ireland agriculture and manufacture were so interconnected 'that many of those who come under the description of farmers, and who actually are such, are also weavers'. And since there was no distinction in dress or appearance between the two groups it was impossible for the inspecting officers to say with any certainty whether the passengers were artisans or not. The consequence was that the Proclamation was virtually a dead letter.[2]

The causes of the continued emigration were to be found in the first place in the depressed state of the Ulster economy. Henry Wansey, an English visitor to New York, boarded a recently arrived emigrant ship from Ireland in 1794 and commented of the passengers:[3]

> I made a point to find many of them out and ask them why they left their country. They told me the times were so hard, and everything so dear, that with all their industry, they could not live. They said that . . . near two hundred of them were weavers of diaper and dimity [and] . . . that most of them were going to the western parts of Connecticut to settle on new lands.

Predominant though economic factors were, it remains true that emigration was further stimulated by the political discontent that led to the formation of the United Irishmen. This was certainly the view of the Collector at Derry, who observed in 1796 that 'though the emigration of useful workmen . . . from a country must be injurious to it, and should if possible be prevented, yet it is to be considered that . . . many of those who leave are of discontented and turbulent dispositions'.[4] The number of emigrants of this description seems to have reached its peak immediately after the failure of the 1798 rebellion. As is well

[1] Ibid, 20 Apl. 1795.
[2] B.M. Addl. MS 33102, pp. 2–4. R. G. Hill to Thos. Pelham, 28 Apl. 1796.
[3] Henry Wansey, *The Journal of an Excursion to the United States of North America in the Summer of 1794* (Salisbury, 1796), pp. 204–5.
[4] B.M. Addl. MS 33102, pp. 2–4. R. G. Hill to Thos. Pelham 28 Apl. 1796.

known many of the leaders of the United Irishmen, including
Emmet, Sampson and MacNeven, made their way to the United
States after varying periods of time. But it was not only the leaders
who emigrated. Thomas Ledlie Birch reported, for example, that
the vessel on which he sailed from Belfast to New York in 1798
was full of political refugees. He added:[1]

> The greater number of us have been literally transported from His
> Britannic Majesty's Dominions under sentence of a Court Martial,
> or obliged to fly to avoid instant death by military execution . . .
> Many hundreds of persons of rank and property are in similar
> situation, and all bent on coming to this Continent, forming the
> most respectable emigration which has taken place to the United
> States since the settlement of the New England Colonies.

It would, however, be wrong to conclude that emigration from
Ulster in the 1790s was composed exclusively of the more self-
sufficient and respectable classes. Along with the artisans, the
prosperous farmers, and the professional men there was a poorer
element whose destitution was beginning to cause concern to
municipal authorities in the United States. Thus when a vessel
from Newry landed 300 passengers at New York in 1796, the
Common Council complained of a 'prodigious influx of indigent
foreigners' and suggested that poor relief should become a state
rather than a municipal responsibility.[2]

However composed, the emigration from Ireland was not to be
allowed to go on without check. Having failed in its efforts to
reduce emigration by a flat prohibition, the British Government
turned to more roundabout methods. The Passenger Act of 1803,[3]
the first of a long series of measures regulating steerage conditions,
severely limited the number of passengers which vessels could
carry to North America and stipulated, among other things, that
adequate supplies of water and provisions be carried for the
voyage. That legislative action was badly needed to regulate the
emigrant traffic is beyond question. In the opinion of one
observer:[4]

---

[1] Thomas Ledlie Birch, *A Letter from an Irish Emigrant to his friend in the United States*
(New York, 1798), p. 1.
[2] *Minutes of the Common Council of the City of New York, 1784–1831*, 19 vols. (New York,
1917), Vol. II, facing p. 212, pp. 263–5, 478, 485, 490–1.
[3] 43 Geo. III, c. 56.
[4] Charles W. Janson, *The Stranger in America, 1793–1806* (New York, 1935), p. 462.

Guinea-man with slaves were never crowded like the American
ships from Londonderry to Philadelphia with Irish passengers.
A small ship of 215 tons took on board 530 passengers . . . being
nearly double the number ever attempted to be stowed in a slave
ship of equal burden.

Nor was overcrowding the only evil, for some of the captains in
the trade were completely indifferent to the welfare of their
passengers. Captain Robert Cunningham, of Londonderry, was,
for example, prosecuted in 1790 in Philadelphia for having failed
to supply his passengers with sufficient food during the voyage.
At the trial, which ended in Cunningham's conviction and in his
being fined £500, it emerged that the passengers had been kept
on short rations for three weeks before the vessel reached the
Delaware, and that it was in a filthy state on arrival.[1]

Yet it may be doubted whether a desire to remedy these un-
doubted abuses represented the real motive for the enactment of
the 1803 Act. A measure of precisely this kind had been advocated
for some time by those who wanted to see emigration restrained.
Thus Phineas Bond had suggested as long ago as 1788 that the
best method of checking emigration would be to introduce regulations so stringent as to make it unprofitable for shipowners to
carry passengers across the Atlantic. According to Bond,[2]

> Such a regulation would steer clear of a direct restraint upon the
> will of the subject to migrate; but would as effectually remedy the
> evil by destroying the means of emigration under colour of a
> humane provision for the comforts of those who are disposed to
> quit their native country.

There is no evidence that, in adopting such regulations, the
British Government had decided to act upon Bond's advice or,
indeed, upon that of Lord Cornwallis who, as Lord Lieutenant of
Ireland, had attempted in 1801 to check Irish emigration by just
such a measure as Bond had proposed.[3] The immediate impetus

---

[1] Erna Risch, 'Immigrant Aid Societies before 1820', *Pennsylvania Magazine of History
and Biography*, Vol. 60, no. 1 (1 Jan. 1936), p. 31.
[2] *Annual Report of the American Historical Association*, 1896, Vol. 1, p. 581. Bond to
Lord Carmarthen, 16 Nov. 1788. Bond repeated the suggestion at intervals throughout the 1790s. See, for example, F.O. 5/10, Bond to Lord Carmarthen, 15 Nov. 1795.
[3] H.O. 100/105. Cornwallis to Commissioners of the Revenue, 22 Apl. 1801.
Cornwallis instructed the Irish Customs Officers to refuse to clear out any vessel

for the adoption of the Passenger Act came neither from the United States nor from Ireland. A committee of the Royal Highland Society, appointed to suggest remedies for the depopulation of the Scottish Highlands, had in 1802 produced a report which, among other things, drew attention to the scandalous condition of emigrant ships leaving Scotland.[1] These revelations appear to have suggested a method of limiting departures and although, in form, the Passenger Act was a humanitarian measure its real purpose, as Castlereagh admitted to John Quincy Adams, was to check emigration.[2] And while the Scottish situation may have inspired the measure, its framers cannot have been unaware of its likely effect on emigration from Ulster.

The Act provided that the number of passengers which could be carried to America from the United Kingdom was to be limited to a fixed proportion of the ship's registered tonnage. British vessels were limited to one passenger for every two tons, and foreign vessels to one for every five tons. Such a distinction was a particular blow to the emigrant trade from the north of Ireland where trade with the United States was conducted largely in American bottoms. Hitherto a typical American vessel of 300 tons had been in the habit of carrying between 300 and 500 passengers on each voyage; but the Passenger Act would permit it in future to carry no more than 60. The immediate consequence of the restriction was a sharp rise in fares. The cost of passage from Londonderry to Philadelphia had until now been about £3. 10*s*., but as soon as the Act came into force it rose to between eight and ten guineas.[3]

For the poorer class of emigrant this was a prohibitive increase. To be sure the Act could in some instances be evaded. One observer wrote in 1807 that 'American ingenuity, added to a little connivance on the part of those who ought to carry the law into effect' had led to the practice of overstating the ship's tonnage.

which had a greater proportion of passengers than one for every 7 tons of the ship's burden. The instructions had to be withdrawn, however, when the Law Officers reported that there was no legal authority to enforce them. *H.O.* 103/3 Portland to Hope, 26 July 1801.

[1] *Parl. Papers*, 1803, Vol. III, part 2. Report from the Committee on the Survey of the Coasts, &c of Scotland, Relating to Emigration, 1803, Appendix A.
[2] Worthington C. Ford (ed.), *The Writings of John Quincy Adams*, 7 vols. (New York, 1913–17), Vol. VI, p. 54.
[3] B.M. Addl. MS 35932. Passengers from Ireland to America, 1803–6.

Thus, one American vessel of 215 tons was recorded at London-derry as one of 400 tons, enabling her to carry almost twice her legal complement.[1] Moreover, it soon became the practice to take on extra passengers after the inspection by the customs officers had taken place, though there was always the risk that the vessel would be intercepted at sea by British cruisers and escorted back to port.[2]

But despite such evasions the Act drastically reduced the volume of Irish emigration. Phineas Bond, reporting from Phila-delphia in 1805, was gratified to be able to assure the Government that the measure he had long advocated had produced precisely the effects he had predicted for it.

> It affords me very High Satisfaction to observe the beneficial effect resulting from the Act . . . regulating the Vessels carrying Pas-sengers from His Majesty's United Kingdom. A great number of Vessels having on board German Passengers arrived in the Dela-ware during last Summer and Autumn; but as to Great Britain and Ireland, the destructive Commerce hither seems to have ceased.[3]

Though this was an exaggerated claim it was an understandable one, bearing in mind the heavy immigration that Bond had witnessed in the previous twenty years.

In the 1780s and 1790s, as we have seen, an annual emigration from Ulster of 5,000 people or more had not been unusual. But the returns made by the Irish Customs Board to London reveal that in the three-year period 1803–5 the total emigration from Ireland was only 3,467, or little more than one thousand a year.[4] These returns were sufficiently detailed to provide a fairly full picture of Irish emigration at this time. They show, for example, that roughly 70 per cent of the emigrants from Ireland in that three-year period sailed from the three leading Ulster ports which had long predominated in the emigrant traffic. Londonderry sent 1,283 emigrants, Belfast 646 and Newry 576; of the other Irish ports only Dublin, with 570, sent an appreciable number. But there had nevertheless been a substantial change since the 1790s, for it was to New York, rather than to Philadelphia, that the majority of emigrant ships now sailed. Of the 100 vessels which,

[1] Janson, *Stranger in America*, pp. 462–3.
[2] *Belfast Monthly Magazine* (July 1811), Vol. VIII, p. 79.
[3] F.O. 5/46. Bond to Harrowby, 4 Mar. 1805.
[4] B.M. Addl. MS 35932. Passengers from Ireland to America, 1803–6.

with their 3,467 passengers, sailed from Ireland for the United States in 1803–5, 58 with 1,855 passengers were bound for New York, 23 with 999 passengers for Philadelphia, Newcastle and Wilmington, while the rest were divided between Baltimore, Charleston and Boston.[1] The substitution of New York for Philadelphia as the main port of arrival should not be taken to mean that emigrants had developed a sudden antipathy to Pennsylvania. What seems to have happened is that New York had now replaced Philadelphia as the main centre of the flaxseed trade—and, indeed, in much else—and emigrants were simply pulled along as usual in the wake of commerce.[2]

The passenger lists of the vessels leaving during these years show that the characteristic pattern of Ulster emigration was in family groups, though there was always a fair sprinkling of un-accompanied single young men. Not much can be learned from the lists about the emigrants' occupations since these were invari-ably recorded as farmers, labourers or spinsters and, as we have seen, such designations often concealed the fact that those departing were actually artisans. Moreover, since the lists make no mention of religion, it is not possible to use them to determine what proportion of the emigrants were Presbyterians. But an examination of the family names of the passengers and of the places from whence they come strongly suggests that they were in fact overwhelmingly Scotch-Irish. This was true even of Lon-donderry, which might have been expected to have a higher pro-portion of Catholic than did Belfast or Newry. A typical passenger list from Londonderry—that of the ship *Ardent*, which sailed for Baltimore on 23 April 1803—reveals the predominance of such characteristically Scotch-Irish surnames as Ramsey, Elliott, Richey, McKee, Clark, McCullough, Montgomery, Graham and Crawford and only one characteristically Catholic Irish name, that of Pat Cunigan.[3]

Reduced in this fashion to a trickle, emigration continued at low

---

[1] These returns are printed in the *New England Historical and Genealogical Register*, Vol. LX, pp. 23–8, 160–4, 240–3, 346–9; LXI, pp. 133–9, 265–70, 347–9; LXIII, pp. 78–81, 168–71; LXVI, pp. 30–2, 306–8.

[2] Robert G. Albion, *The Rise of New York Port, 1815–1860* (New York and London, 1939), p. 8; Herbert Heaton, 'The American Trade', in C. Northcote Parkinson (ed.), *The Trade Winds: A Study of British Overseas Trade during the French Wars, 1793–1815* (London, 1948), p. 204.

[3] *New England Historical and Genealogical Register*, Vol. LX (Apl. 1906), pp. 163–4.

ebb throughout the Napoleonic Wars. The authorities not only made strenuous attempts to enforce the Passenger Act but showed its hostility to emigration in other ways. 'The Government', it was reported from Londonderry in 1811, 'appears to give every discouragement to the trade of emigration and to throw every obstacle in the way of going out short of passing an Act absolutely to prohibit it.'[1] Periods of scarcity gave the authorities new pretexts for action and, on the grounds that food could not be exported, shipmasters were forbidden at times to lay in provisions for American-bound passenger ships.

Emigration was, however, becoming not only more difficult but more hazardous. Even those who managed to embark for the United States faced the risk of being intercepted on the high seas by short-handed British warships on the lookout for likely recruits. The impressment of seamen from American merchantmen during the French wars is, of course, a familiar story. Less well known is the fact that considerable numbers of Irish emigrants suffered the same fate while on their way to America.

The practice of impressing emigrants began quite early during the struggle with France. One of the earliest victims was the American ship *Cincinnatus* which, in the summer of 1795, was carrying 300 passengers on a voyage from Belfast to Philadelphia. Among the passengers was Wolfe Tone, who later described his encounter with the Royal Navy as follows:

> Some time after we cleared the banks of Newfoundland, we were stopped by three British frigates, the *Thetis*, Capt. Lord Cochrane, the *Hussar*, Capt. Rose, and the *Esperance*, Capt. Wood, who boarded us and, after treating us with the greatest insolence . . . they pressed every one of our hands save one, and near fifty of my fellow-passengers, who were most of them flying to avoid the tyranny of a bad government at home, and who thus most unexpectedly fell under the severest tyranny . . . which exists. As I was in a jacket and trowsers, one of the lieutenants ordered me into the boat as a fit man to serve the king, and it was only the screams of my wife and sister which induced him to desist.[2]

Cases of impressment of emigrant passengers became more

---

[1] *The Shamrock or Hibernian Chronicle* (New York), 26 Oct. 1811, quoting the *Belfast Monthly Magazine*, n.d.
[2] William Theobald Wolfe Tone (ed.), *Life of Theobald Wolfe Tone*, 2 vols. (Washington, D.C., 1826), Vol. II, p. 130.

frequent after the war with France was resumed in 1803,[1] and reached a climax in the period immediately before the outbreak of the War of 1812. In the twelve months before war was declared, at least thirteen emigrant ships from Ireland were intercepted by British warships and nearly 200 of their passengers were impressed. Most of the interceptions took place off Long Island or the Capes of the Delaware so that emigrants were snatched away from their families when almost in sight of the American coast.[2]

Such events produced a violent reaction from Irish-American newspapers, one of which denounced the impressment of emigrants as 'an abominable outrage on justice, liberty and humanity'.[3] In Ireland itself indignation at the practice was no less intense, particularly after an incident which took place, not on the high seas, but in the supposed security of an Irish harbour. In May 1812 four American vessels, having embarked their full legal complements of passengers at Londonderry, had anchored in Moville Bay before proceeding to sea when the British armed schooner *Barbara* appeared in search of hands. Boarding parties were sent to each of the American vessels, and a total of 150 emigrants was carried off. When the news reached Londonderry it produced a sensation, and a meeting of merchants was convened to condemn 'this disgraceful transaction'. Petitions were sent to the Lord Lieutenant and to the Lords of the Admiralty, and eventually the impressed men were released. But by this time war with America had broken out and the emigrants were unable to join their families in America.[4]

The obstacles placed in the path of emigration by Parliament and the Royal Navy respectively were all the more resented by Irish shipping interests because transatlantic commerce already had been badly affected by the commercial restrictions adopted successively by the United States from 1807 onward in an effort to induce the European belligerents to respect the maritime rights of neutrals. These restrictions had had a curious effect on emigration, first checking it and then facilitating it. The Jeffersonian

---

[1] *Federal Gazette and Baltimore Daily Advertiser*, 15 May 1806.
[2] *Shamrock*, 6 July, 10 Aug., 23 Dec. 1811, 12 June 1812; *Western Star and Harp of Erin* (Boston), 26 May, 20, 27 June, 18, 25 July, 1 Aug. 1812.
[3] *Western Star*, 20 June 1812.
[4] *B.N.L.*, 29 May 1812; *Adm.* 1/4221. Saxton to Croker, 28 May 1812 and enclosures, 2, 12 June 1812; *Adm.* 1/4222. Saxton to Croker, 17 July 1812, Schoales to Croker, 14 July 1812.

embargo, in force between December 1807 and March 1809, had forbidden American vessels to go abroad and had all but shut American ports to British ships. This had meant that in 1808 the only vessels available for carrying emigrants from Ireland were a few American ships returning home, and they had room for only a few hundred passengers. The Non-Importation policy, on the other hand, had the opposite effect since large numbers of American vessels, forbidden to load their usual cargoes at Liverpool, crossed over to Ireland in the hope of securing emigrants. The result was that in 1811 and 1812 the volume of emigration was greater than it had been for a decade. In 1811, 55 emigrant ships carried out a total of 3,500 passengers, mainly from the ports of Londonderry, Belfast, Newry and Dublin. In the following year, more than 2,000 passengers had left by July when news was received of the American declaration of war.[1]

The war of 1812 once more meant a break in the flow of emigrants. But in the thirty years that had elapsed since the United States had become independent, perhaps 100,000 people from Ulster had settled there. Many of them joined their friends and relatives in the Scotch-Irish settlements established earlier in Pennsylvania, Virginia and the Carolinas. But a significant number settled in the cities of the eastern seaboard, especially Philadelphia, Baltimore and New York.[2] This tended to be the case particularly of the professional men who emigrated in such numbers during this period.

The growth of these urban Scotch-Irish settlements was, of course, a new phenomenon and it was to have important political consequences. The 1790s were a period of violent political agitation in the United States, with opinion sharply divided on the issue of the French Revolution. In the conflict between Federalists and Republicans, the Scotch-Irish were overwhelmingly on the side of the Jeffersonians, whose sympathies were with Republican France. Not only did Scotch-Irish immigrants share these sympathies, but they instinctively hated the Federalists as would-be aristocrats and as tools of the British. Taking advantage of the wider opportunities for political activity afforded by their urban concentration, the Scotch-Irish plunged at once into the political

---

[1] Heaton, 'The American Trade', pp. 215, 222, 223 n.; *Shamrock*, 1811, *passim*.
[2] W. F. Adams, *Ireland and Irish Emigration to the New World from 1815 to the Famine* (New Haven, 1932), pp. 351–2.

fray, becoming prominent in the newly formed Democratic-Republican clubs and in Republican militia units.[1]

The Scotch-Irish were especially prominent in the agitation against Jay's Treaty, which in Republican eyes made too many concessions to Britain. At a mass meeting in Philadelphia in July 1795, one of the city's leading merchants, the Ulster-born Blair McClenachan, urged his audience to 'kick this damned treaty to hell'. Then, placing a copy of the document upon a pole, he led a mob to the house of the British minister, where the treaty was ceremonially burned.[2] Among those present at the meeting was Archibald Hamilton Rowan, who had arrived in the United States only three days before and had thus lost no time in demonstrating an interest in American politics. But Rowan, like two other leaders of the United Irishmen, Wolfe Tone and Napper Tandy, proved to be less an immigrant than an exile; during their brief stay in the United States, they were to be less concerned with American politics than with planning a return to Ireland.[3]

But another prominent United Irishman, Dr James Reynolds, remained in America for the rest of his life and became one of Philadelphia's best-known Jeffersonian Republicans. Dr Reynolds is a significant figure in the emigration of this period. A physician from Cookstown, County Tyrone,[4] he was prominent in the Dungannon Convention,[5] and in March 1793 he was summoned before the Irish House of Lords to give an account of his activities. He refused, however, to be examined on oath, declaring that the House of Lords had no judicial powers, and for his contumacy he was imprisoned for five months.[6] In 1794 he was one of those United Irishmen who became involved in secret negotiations with France, and, learning that he was about to be arrested, fled to America.[7] On the vessel which took him from Belfast to Phila-

---

[1] John C. Miller, *Crisis in Freedom: The Alien and Sedition Acts* (Boston, 1952), pp. 41 ff.
[2] George Gibbs, *Memoirs of the Administrations of Washington and John Adams . . .*, 2 vols. (New York, 1846), Vol. I, p. 217.
[3] Tone, *Life of Theobald Wolfe Tone*, Vol. I, p. 131.
[4] R. B. McDowell, 'The Personnel of the Dublin Society of United Irishmen, 1791–4', *Irish Historical Studies*, Vol. II (1940–1), p. 45.
[5] R. B. McDowell, *Irish Public Opinion, 1750–1800* (London, 1944), pp. 189–90.
[6] Rosamund Jacob, *The Rise of the United Irishmen, 1791–1794* (London, 1937), p. 142.
[7] D. A. Chart, *The Drennan Letters* (Belfast, 1931), pp. 106, 209; Historical Manuscripts Commission, *Thirteenth Report* (London, 1894), Charlemont MS, Vol. II, p. 244.

delphia he made his political sentiments plain beyond question by hanging an effigy of George III from the yardarm, and by treating his fellow-passengers and the crew to glasses of rum with which to 'drink to the confusion of despots and the prosperity of liberty all the world over'.[1]

Settling in Philadelphia, Dr Reynolds wasted no time in plunging into political agitation. His American career was comparatively short—he died in 1808[2]—but it was rarely free from controversy. Having induced a leading Republican editor to publish a story accusing the Federalist Secretary of State, Timothy Pickering, of accepting bribes, Reynolds found himself in 1798 sued for libel.[3] Then in the following year, so vigorously did he lead the agitation against the Alien and Sedition Acts that he was prosecuted for seditious riot.[4] A few years later he was a protagonist in one of the leading medical controversies of the day, that concerning the origins of yellow fever;[5] and in 1807 his removal from the Philadelphia Board of Health became a leading issue in the impeachment of the Governor of Pennsylvania, Thomas McKean.[6] Nor does this exhaust the catalogue of Reynolds's activities for, amidst all his tribulations, he found time to write the first Utopian novel to appear in the United States—a work published in 1802 under the significant title of *Equality*.[7]

Reynolds was, of course, only one of the most prominent members of that group of Scotch-Irish immigrants who became Jefferson's enthusiastic supporters. Indeed, it was the alliance between the Republicans and the Scotch-Irish that convinced the Federalists of the necessity of disfranchising immigrants. 'If some

[1] Alexander B. Grosart (ed.), *The Poems and Literary Prose of Alexander Wilson*, (4 vols. Paisley, 1876), Vol. I, pp. 59–62.
[2] George W. Corner, *The Autobiography of Benjamin Rush* (Princeton, 1948), p. 322 and n.
[3] Octavius Pickering and C. W. Upham, *The Life of Timothy Pickering*, (4 vols. Boston, 1867–73), Vol. III, pp. 307–10; Raymond Walters, jr., *Alexander James Dallas* (Philadelphia, 1942), p. 133.
[4] Francis Wharton, *State Trials of the United States during the Administrations of Washington and Adams* (Philadelphia, 1849), pp. 345–91.
[5] Frederick P. Henry (ed.), *Standard History of the Medical Profession of Philadelphia* (Chicago, 1897), pp. 118–19.
[6] Sanford W. Higginbotham, *The Keystone in the Democratic Arch: Pennsylvania Politics, 1800–1816* (Harrisburg, Pa., 1952), pp. 126–7.
[7] The work first appeared in serial form in the columns of a Philadelphia Deist newspaper, *The Temple of Reason*, and has since been republished twice. See A.C.P. (ed.), *Equality: A History of Lithconia* (Philadelphia, 1947), pp. v–vi.

means are not adopted to prevent the indiscriminate admission of wild Irishmen and others to the right of suffrage', wrote Harrison Gray Otis of Massachusetts, 'there will soon be an end to liberty and property.'[1] Uriah Tracy of Connecticut took a similar view after a lengthy journey through the Scotch-Irish settlements in Pennsylvania. 'With a very few exceptions', wrote Tracy, 'they are United Irishmen, Free Masons, and the most God-provoking Democrats this side of Hell.'[2]

Federalist hostility culminated in an attempt in 1798 to deprive the Republicans of their supply of foreign-born voters. A revised Naturalisation Act was adopted, lengthening from five years to fourteen the minimum period of residence needed to qualify for American citizenship. The purpose of the measure, according to Otis, was to debar from citizenship 'the mass of vicious and disorganising characters who cannot live peaceably at home, and who, after unfurling the standard of rebellion in their own country, . . . come here to revolutionise ours'.[3]

At the same time the Adams Administration took steps to prevent any further immigration of Irish revolutionaries. The British Government was prepared to release several of those who had participated in the 1798 rebellion on condition that they went abroad permanently. But when Emmet, MacNeven and Sampson accepted the offer and signified their intention of emigrating to the United States, the American Minister in London, Rufus King, intervened to stop them. He informed the British Government that the United States wanted no more Irish rebels who would 'arrange themselves on the side of the malcontents'. In consequence the offer was withdrawn and Emmet and his companions had to spend several years longer in gaol.[4]

Ironically enough, each of these Federalist measures was to recoil upon its authors. Many of the rebels denied admission to the United States in 1798 made their way there nevertheless within a few years, and, once there, played an important part in thwarting King's political ambitions. When he ran for the governorship of New York in 1807, and again when he was the Federalist candidate for the presidency in 1816, Emmet and

[1] S. E. Morison, *The Life and Letters of Harrison Gray Otis, Federalist, 1765–1848*, (Boston, 1913), Vol. I, p. 107. 2 vols.
[2] Gibbs, *Memoirs*, Vol. II, p. 399.
[3] Morison, *Otis*, Vol. I, p. 108.
[4] Carl Wittke, *The Irish in America* (Baton Rouge, La., 1956), pp. 79–80.

Sampson rallied their countrymen against him by reminding them of what King had done in 1798.[1] Moreover, the Naturalisation Act of 1798 transformed Scotch-Irish suspicion of the Federalists into implacable opposition. In common with other immigrant groups, Scotch-Irish voters turned out in their thousands in 1800 to elect Jefferson, and their influence may have been decisive. New York was the hinge upon which the whole election turned, and one observer testified that Jefferson carried the state only because of the mass support he received in New York City from Scotch-Irish and French voters.[2]

Just as in the colonial and Revolutionary periods, therefore, Scotch-Irish immigrants exercised an important political influence from the moment they set foot in America. Not that they were the only natives of Ireland to do so. In the 1812 presidential election, for example, the chief spokesmen for the rival candidates, Madison[3] and De Witt Clinton, were respectively Thomas Addis Emmet and John Binns, both of whom were Irish-born but not Ulstermen. But it was mainly the Scotch-Irish, rather than immigrants from southern Ireland, who provided Emmet and Binns with the support they needed to rise to political leadership. What is striking about the group-consciousness of this period, indeed, is that immigrants from every part of Ireland shared a sense of fellow-feeling. Later on, when the issues of Catholic Emancipation were to arise, and anti-Catholicism was to become an important strain in American nativism, old animosities would be reawakened and both the Scotch-Irish and the Catholic Irish would insist upon their distinctiveness. But for the moment both groups were content to be simply Irishmen, collaborating in politics, sharing newspapers like the New York *Shamrock*, and joining together in such benevolent organisations as the Friendly Sons of St Patrick.

What brought this chapter of Scotch-Irish emigration to a close was, of course, the war of 1812, an event which might have presented a conflict of loyalties to recent arrivals from the United Kingdom. But there was never any doubt of the American loyalties of the newcomers from Ulster. The tradition of hostility to

[1] George Potter, *To the Golden Door* (Boston, 1960), pp. 220–1.
[2] Eugene P. Link, *Democratic-Republican Societies, 1790–1800* (New York, 1942), p. 87.
[3] Irving Brant, *James Madison, Commander-in-Chief, 1812–1836* (Indianapolis, 1961), pp. 107–8.

England, so marked during the Revolution, had received fresh stimulus from the failure of the 1798 rebellion and from the practice of impressment. Thus when the war of 1812 broke out, the Scotch-Irish came down unhesitatingly on the side of their adopted country, and some of them took a leading part in resisting the British army which set fire to Washington in 1814.[1]

The war was to end with a smashing American victory in the battle of New Orleans, in which Wellington's veterans were overwhelmed by an army led by Andrew Jackson, who was the first American of Scotch-Irish stock to become President. Jackson, born on the Carolina frontier in 1767 of Scotch-Irish parents, represented the older Scotch-Irish strain in America, as did John C. Calhoun and others who were now rising to prominence in American political life. But such men thought of themselves as Americans rather than Scotch-Irishmen, and so for that matter did such representatives of the newer Scotch-Irish element as William Sampson and David Baillie Warden who had not been born in America. A common loyalty to America was, however, only one of the things that united Scotch-Irish 'colonists' with Scotch-Irish 'immigrants'. The two groups had left Ireland for much the same reasons; they had settled in roughly the same areas in the United States; they shared not only the same religious faith but common political beliefs. They almost certainly made no distinction among themselves between those who had arrived in American before 1776 and those who had followed later. Historians, looking back at the exodus from Ulster from the perspective of the twentieth century, may well feel it to be time to follow their example and to regard the story of Scotch-Irish emigration as one which transcends the familiar landmarks of American political history.

---

[1] Thomas D'Arcy McGee, *A History of the Irish Settlers in America* (Boston, 1852), pp. 104–5.

CHAPTER IV

The Scotch-Irish: Their Cultural Adaptation and Heritage in the American Old West[1]

by E. Estyn Evans

The history of the Scotch-Irish in colonial and republican North America has been written largely in terms of their individual contributions and in the light of outmoded concepts of racial distinctiveness. The older literature, at least, is strongly coloured by hero-worship or by prejudice, and paints a picture that is either white or black. While the descendants of the eighteenth-century immigrants have applauded this 'bold and hardy race' (the phrase is Theodore Roosevelt's) for its massive contributions to leadership in American life—in the political, educational, religious, military and industrial fields—some English writers have stressed the depravity of a stock which they see mainly as backwoodsmen producing little more than gangsters, hill-billies and bad whiskey. An English farmer visiting America about the year 1800 wrote: 'None emigrate to the frontiers beyond the mountains, except culprits, or savage backwoodsmen, chiefly of Irish descent . . . a race possessing all the vices of civilised and savage life, without

[1] The substance of this address has been published in three articles: 'The Scotch-Irish in the New World; An Atlantic Heritage' (*Journ. Roy. Soc. Antiquaries of Ireland* 35 (1965), pp. 39–49); 'Culture and Land Use in the Old West of North America' (*Festgabe für Gottfried Pfeifer: Heidelberg Geographische Arbeiten* 15 (1966), pp. 72–80); 'Cultural Relics of the Ulster-Scots in the Old West of North America', *Ulster Folklife* 11 (1965), pp. 33–8. I am grateful to the editors of these journals for permission to use material and illustrations from these articles. I wish in addition to express my thanks to several friends in the U.S.A. for their help in discussion and field study in various parts of North America east of the Mississippi, particularly to Professors Fred Kniffen, J. Fraser Hart and Gary Dunbar and Mr Henry Glassie. My thanks are also due to Miss Eileen Duncan, Department of Geography, Queen's University, Belfast, for preparing the two maps.

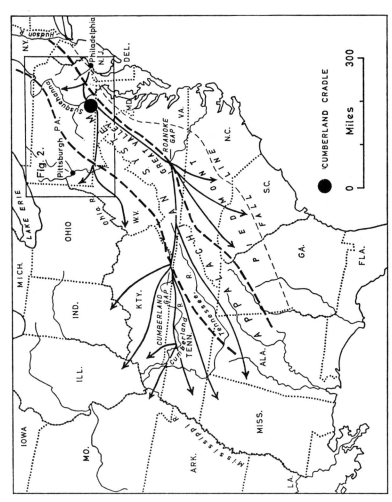

Fig. 1 Lines of Expansion of Ulster Immigrants from the Cumberland Cradle.

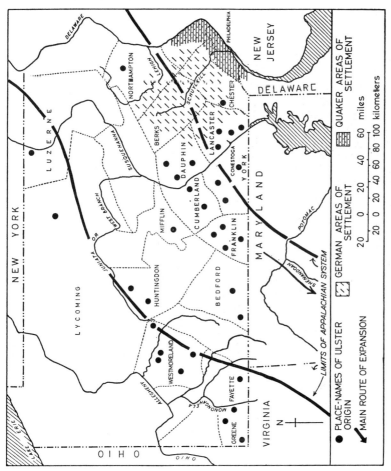

Fig. 2 Scotch-Irish Settlement in Pennsylvania.

the virtues of either . . . the outcasts of the world, and the disgrace of it. They are to be met with, on the western frontiers, from Pennsylvania inclusive, to the furthest south.'[1] More recently Arnold Toynbee, to prove his theory of 'challenge and response', convinced himself that the Scotch-Irish 'succumbed to the barbarising severity of their Appalachian environment' and became 'no better than barbarians, the American counterparts of the Hairy Ainu'.[2] The opinions of a contemporary observer and a theoretical historian have this in common: they are the views of Englishmen and reflect the cultural attitudes of a people accustomed to the ordered life of law-abiding villages and urban centres; and the Scotch-Irish were successful pioneers precisely because they could live without the benefits, and actively opposed the restrictions, of organised community life. Denigration of a different kind has come from the descendants of Irish Roman Catholic immigrants in the United States, though this view, too, has been coloured by the scorn of a newly urbanised stock for old rural values.

Those Americans who claim Scotch-Irish ancestry—and they are many—seem to have no doubt as to the superior qualities of their ancestors. The Proceedings of the Scotch-Irish Congress, published from 1889 onwards, are full of such immoderate self-praise and self-righteousness that one may perhaps count among the contributions of this stock the traditional boastfulness as well as the isolationism of the American Middle West. They were not alone, however, in their extravagant ancestral claims, for other descendants of old immigrant groups were vociferous during the half-century before the First World War, when they felt themselves in danger of being swamped by floods of impoverished European immigrants.[3] The Scotch-Irish in particular were anxious not to be confused with the 'famine Irish', and the term Scotch-Irish significantly became popular only after 1850: before that they were usually referred to as Irish (sometimes wild Irish) or poor Scotch. But these non-English groups, and particularly

---

[1] William Strickland, *Observations on the Agriculture of the United States of America*, London, 1801, p. 71.
[2] Arnold Toynbee, *A Study of History*, Vol. 2 (1934), pp. 302, 311.
[3] The Pennsylvania-German Society started its publication in 1891. The Scotch-Irish Society of America, founded in 1889, seems to have grown out of a meeting held in Belfast *c.* 1884, at which Professor George Macloskie and President McCosh of Princeton University were present.

The Scotch-Irish: Their Cultural Adaptation

the Scotch-Irish, also found a grievance in the fact that American history had been mainly written in New England[1] and that this interpretation of its course reflected the old English conviction of cultural superiority. In assessing the fundamental contributions of various immigrant cultures it must be said that the town meeting and the cherished right of free speech were essentially the gifts of the urban New Englanders.[2] The territorial unit—the township —also spread from New England.

The Scotch-Irish propagandists, in Ulster as well as in America, have weakened the force of their claims to have provided outstanding leaders in so many walks of American life by laying stress on quantity and by including in their lists of pioneers and presidents some men of doubtful virtue and others whose qualities could conceivably have been derived from a father or a mother of lesser breed.[3] If the important part played by the Scotch-Irish in the American Revolution, in the shaping of the Old Frontier and in political leadership, cannot be denied, there is equally no doubt that, ironically, Scotch-Irish relics are today a substantial element in the depressed rural population of Appalachia, which legislation inspired by the concept of the New Frontier is designed to rehabilitate.

But it is not my purpose to follow either of these historic trails or to judge which should be given greater weight in assessing the role of the Scotch-Irish in the life of the United States. It is my contention that their major lasting contribution to the American scene was their broad imprint on the American landscape and way of life. It can be fairly claimed that, all in all, the middle colonies were the most significant cultural nursery of North America, thanks to the hybridisation of the various cultural groups which were attracted to Penn's colony. Growing out of it, southern and western Pennsylvania which the Scotch-Irish so largely fashioned became in turn the cradle of the Middle West. The family-farm and the family-bible were the foundations of faith. The dignity of the individual was valued and distinctions of class were scorned. The cultural landscape of a large part of the United States is characterised by the single homestead and the unincorporated

[1] Charles A. Hanna, *The Scotch-Irish*, Vol. 1 (1902), p. 1.
[2] J. G. Leyburn, *The Scotch-Irish: A Social History*, 1962, p. 316.
[3] On this topic see Leyburn (op. cit., p. 315), who gives a fair summary of the divergent views held about the Scotch-Irish.

hamlet, and by a system of land-use dominated by a corn-and-livestock economy, which was pioneered in the Old West mainly by the Scotch-Irish. Among them the claims of family and kin were stronger than those of community. Economically, it was a wasteful system, often bringing rapid environmental deterioration. They were militant moralists, and free enterprise was raised to the level of a theological dogma. While Presbyterianism tended to become schismatic or to give way to the more emotional appeal of the Methodists and Baptists as the settlers moved ahead of established churches, its adherents clung to the ideal of an educated clergy and must be given some of the credit for the American passion for education. Of the 207 permanent colleges established in the United States before the Civil War about 50—by far the largest single group—were begun by Presbyterians, mostly of Ulster ancestry.[1] Their critics averred, however, that they believed in education only if they controlled it.

The fact that the Scotch-Irish constituted a high proportion of the first European farmers (as distinct from traders and adventurers) in the American wilderness helps to explain their formative role, for pioneers set a pattern that tends to persist. Their trails become roads: their system of settlement and land-use is stamped on the landscape. Some features of frontier life are universal, and the Scotch-Irish backwoodsmen displayed them not because of their vaunted 'racial' attributes but simply because they lived the life of the frontier. Frontier conditions make for independence, masculine dominance, lawlessness, superstition, improvisation and inventiveness. The first version of the McCormick reaper, for example, was evolved in Virginia in the early 1830s. The question that has to be asked, then, is how the Ulster immigrants came to be so numerous among the pioneers who penetrated into the wilderness.

This is explained partly by opportunity—and here the facts are not in dispute—and partly by their experience in Ulster and their cultural inheritance. Some writers lay stress on their stern Presbyterian faith and their determination to practise it without interference, but I attach more importance to their material culture and total way of life. (It must be said, however, that the ready-made organisation of the Presbyterian Church was to stand them in good stead in their fight for political democracy.) The Ulstermen

[1] J. G. Leyburn, op. cit., p. 321.

landed in large numbers in the Delaware ports from 1724 onwards, and since the coastal strip had been pre-empted by William Penn's Quaker followers, mainly English and Welsh, and German Protestant refugees were beginning to settle the country immediately behind, many of them crossed the Susquehanna and settled in Cumberland County, which was to become their main cradle in the New World (Fig. 1). The townships of Antrim, Armagh, Derry, Fermanagh and Tyrone were established here. There were hostile Indians and French to the west, but the Cumberland Valley lies within the great Appalachian ridge and valley complex, so that the opportunity for linear penetration presented itself, southwards down the Shenandoah Valley into the Great Valley of Virginia and beyond. Because German settlers were already in possession of the east side of the Great Valley, they pushed down the western side. Outside southern Pennsylvania they rarely give their settlements Ulster names and cannot therefore be traced by place-names, but the name Cumberland apparently went with them, over the gap of that name, into the Cumberland Valley of Tennessee, which became their second seed-bed. Some 300,000 pioneers poured through the Cumberland Gap between 1775 and 1800.

The immigrants from Ulster had first sought refuge in New England, especially from 1717 to 1720, but they had a bad reception, and were described as 'uncleanly, unwholesome and disgusting'.[1] In New England they were a small minority, though here too they made a characteristic contribution as Indian-fighters and pioneers.[2] From 1724 onwards Philadelphia and the other Delaware ports took the bulk of the Ulster-Scots, and the tide of immigration, slackening after 1730, reached its high point in 1772–3 and thereafter ebbed away as the colonies moved towards political independence.[3] By the end of the century a quarter of a million people—one-sixth of the total European population of the U.S.A.—claimed Scotch-Irish descent, and a considerable proportion of them had already crossed the Appalachians. Even the tolerant Quakers of Philadelphia found the Ulstermen un-

[1] J. G. Leyburn, op. cit., p. 152.
[2] D. McCourt, 'County Derry and New England', *County Londonderry Handbook*, 1964, pp. 87–101.
[3] The fullest and most recent survey is R. J. Dickson, *Ulster Emigration to Colonial America, 1718–1775*, 1966.

couth and subversive, 'a pernicious and pugnacious people',[1] but
as pacifists the Quakers were willing to find room for fighters on
the unsettled Indian frontier. The Ulstermen, not unwilling to go
where they could take land at little or no financial cost, were also
attracted by the prospect of finding freedom from established
authority. And they were apparently not hindered by their
women-folk, who, in patriarchal subordination, submitted to the
ordeals of frontier life and repeated uprootings.

Their German neighbours, the Pennsylvania 'Dutch', already
20,000 strong by 1727, were also settled in south-eastern Pennsylvania—mainly between the Scotch-Irish and the Quakers
(Fig. 2)—and some of them took part in the drive into the
wilderness, but in general their attitudes were in sharp contrast
to those of the Scotch-Irish. They tended to consolidate their
position while the Scotch-Irish became dispersed. An extreme
example of their resistance to change is provided by the Old
Order Amish, a religious sect which originated in the Emmenthal
and took its name from the Swiss Jacob Amman. The Amish,
who first settled in Pennsylvania in 1727, still largely reject the
modern world in deed as well as word, retaining almost un-
changed their picturesque dress, their agricultural practices—
including their horses and other farm gear—as well as the values
of their eighteenth-century ancestors. Though technologically
fossilised they are excellent farmers and have done so well that
they now occupy much of the country around the lower Susquehanna originally settled by the Scotch-Irish.[2] All the German-
speaking immigrants were Protestants of various kinds, mainly
from the Rhineland and Switzerland, and the many sects formed
endogamous groups which clung together and did not encourage
lone rangers. Their settlements included villages such as Beth-
lehem and they shared with the Scotch-Irish towns such as
Lancaster—which was to become by 1800 the largest 'inland'
town in the United States—and though they increasingly established themselves in separate farms, these were not widely
scattered and the settlements retained something of the cohesion
of village communities. Like the Scotch-Irish they were much

---

[1] Quoted in *Proc. of the First Scotch-Irish Congress, Columbia, Tennessee*, Cincinnati,
1889, p. 184.
[2] The Old Order Amish numbered 43,000 in the U.S.A. in 1960, over half of them
living in Lancaster County.

Abandoned log-cabin of Scotch-Irish type, with half-dovetail cornering, near Bloomington, Indiana

Hewn logs and chinking of cabin of Scotch-Irish type, near Bloomington, Indiana

Stone house with gable-chimney, possibly of Scotch-Irish ancestry, in Oley Valley, Bucks County, Pennsylvania

Abandoned log-cabin, Albemarle County, Virginia. The hillside site is typical of Scotch-Irish settlements

Single farms with patch-cultivation on the Virginia Piedmont near Charlottesville, 1964

given to religion and inured to toil, but unlike them they are said to have been diligent, cheerful, well-mannered, co-operative and law abiding. Skilful farmers, they were also highly skilled in the many arts and crafts which contributed to their needs. They were accustomed to a varied diet and to oven-baked bread, to elaborate equipment for cheese-making, for smoking meat and storing fruit.[1] Their most celebrated champion was Dr Benjamin Rush who called upon the citizens of the Republic to copy the Germans in their 'knowledge and industry in agriculture and manu-factures'.[2] Benjamin Rush was of Scotch-Irish background and it has been claimed that he praised the Germans in order to win them over to American nationalism.[3] Yet, partly because of their alien German tongue, their part in the affairs of the young Republic cannot be compared with that of the English planter-politicians or the Scotch-Irish backwoodsmen. Not until our own century did a Hoover or an Eisenhower, become President of the United States. Their material contributions, however, were con-siderable, and any assessment of the role of the middle colonies in the making of America must take account of the German element.[4] They gave the backwoods the log-cabin, the Kentucky rifle and the Conestoga wagon. The Appalachian dulcimer and perhaps the covered bridge were among their contributions to American 'folklore'.

In time the log-houses and barns of the early German settle-ments were replaced by stone or timber-framed houses and by the vast painted barns (the Switzer barn) which today dominate the rural landscape of the 'Dutch Country' and by means of which

[1] Dr James T. Lemon, 'The Agricultural Practices of National Groups in eighteenth-century south-eastern Pennsylvania', *The Geog. Review*, Vol. 56 (1966), pp. 467–96, refutes these claims. Basing his findings on studies of tax lists and estate inventories, he claims that there were no major differences in farming practice between the Germans and the Scotch-Irish, and that the Germans were no more virtuous in their habits than other immigrants. Folkways, however, are not revealed by statistics, and Dr Lemon does not examine the causes and consequences of expansion outside Pennsylvania. Yet he is probably right in thinking that the contrasted pictures portrayed in contemporary accounts of German and Scotch-Irish settlers were influenced by English stereotypes of the two stocks.
[2] Benjamin Rush, 'An Account of the Manners of the German inhabitants of Pennsylvania', *Columbian Magazine*, Vol. 3 (1789), pp. 22–30.
[3] See Letters of Benjamin Rush (ed. L. H. Butterfield), *Memoirs Amer. Phil. Soc.*, Vol. 30 (1951), p. 368.
[4] A pioneer work, concerned with material culture as well as with political ideas and values, is T. J. Wertenbaker, *The Founding of American Civilization: the Middle Colonies*, 1938.

German expansion in the nineteenth century can be traced through Ohio and Indiana. Almost from the beginning the log-house, or the log-cabin as it came to be called, was adopted by the Scotch-Irish backwoodsmen, and it is to them more than any other group of immigrants that it owes its wide diffusion and its fame. It became so encrusted with sentiment and associated with the shrines of grass-roots politicians of the nineteenth century that one discovers with a shock that, as recently as 1939, there were over 270,000 log-houses still inhabited in the U.S.A., mostly in the Old West.[1] The origin of the American log-cabin has been much discussed. For long erroneously associated with early English tidewater settlements,[2] it was later attributed to the Swedes, and indeed the Swedes settled on the Delaware were probably the first builders of log-houses in America, but it was a German version, as might be guessed, that was taken over by the Scotch-Irish. Henry Glassie,[3] who has made extensive field studies of log constructions, describes the two main techniques of corner timbering used by the Pennsylvania Dutch, leaving aside the simple saddle-notching normally employed for temporary structures. They are V-notching and full dovetailing. The former predominates in the Shenandoah Valley, where there were many Germans, but as one moves further into the Appalachians a modified dovetail—the half dovetail—makes its appearance, and beyond, both in the Blue Ridge country and far to the west of the mountains in Kentucky, Tennessee, Ohio, Indiana, Illinois, Missouri and Arkansas, this method of cornering predominates. Hewn hardwood logs were used, and the interstices between them were filled by 'chinking' with mud, stones or slivers of wood (Pl. 3ii). When the filling is coated with lime-mortar the effect is that of horizontal black-and-white half-

---

[1] *The Farm-housing Survey* (Dept. of Agr. Miscellaneous Publication, no. 323), Washington, 1939.

[2] The myth was exploded by H. L. Shurtleff. See his book *The Log Cabin Myth* (ed. by S. E. Morison), Cambridge, Mass., 1939.

[3] Mr Glassie has very kindly deposited a copy of his Master's thesis, *Southern Mountain Houses: a study in American Folk Culture* (submitted to the State University of New York College in 1965), in the library of the Department of Geography, Queen's University, Belfast. His study of 'The Types of the Southern Mountain Cabin' has now been published as Appendix C in Jan Harold Brunvard, *The Study of American Folklore*, New York, 1968.

See also Fred Kniffen and Henry Glassie, 'Building in Wood in the Eastern United States', *The Geog. Review*, Vol. 56 (1966), pp. 40–66; and Fred Kniffen, 'North American Folk Housing', *Annals of the Ass. of Am. Geog.*, Vol. 55 (1965), pp. 549–77.

timbering. There is a strong Ulster flavour about the remark made by a Tennessee countryman, that 'the man who can make mud which will stick between the logs even if thrown from a distance is as proud as the man who is an expert with the broadaxe'.[1] In the nineteenth century weather-boarding did away with the need for efficient chinking or nogging, and one would not suspect that many houses so boarded over are in fact log-houses. Nearly half the rural houses in some Appalachian counties are said to be log built.

That this variety of log-house can be associated with the Scotch-Irish is attested in other ways: not only is the ground plan almost identical with that of the traditional small Ulster farmhouse, but like the north Ulster house it was generally provided with two opposite doors, and even the half-door was formerly common.[2] The chimney was placed in one of the gables, but whereas in Ireland it is invariably built inside the gable, in the log-house, probably because of the risk of fire, it was built outside in English fashion. The average internal dimensions of this type of log-house are 16 ft by 22 ft, which compares closely with an average of 15 ft by 21 ft for the traditional Ulster kitchen: the external dimensions in fact are almost identical. (The log-cabin adopted by the English settlers who spread into the mountains from tidewater was typically about 16 ft square, reproducing the dimensions of the English single-bay cottage.[3] Although the length and weight of individual logs placed a natural limit on the size of a cabin, it seems clear that the shape of these constructional units—termed pens or cribs—was partly determined by the previous experience of the builders. The immigrants from Ulster had been accustomed to live in rectangular houses whose ground plans were derived from the cruck-roofed house, presumably imported from Scotland. In the eighteenth century, when the Irish woodlands had been largely destroyed, the walls were built of mud or stone or a mixture of both, and the roof was presumably carried on composite cruck-trusses or on coupled rafters resting on the walls, but even where the roof was 'coupled' the restrictions which cruck-construction had placed on the width and height of the house persisted. The single room, though it may have had a small

[1] Henry Glassie, op. cit., p. 73.
[2] W. R. Dunaway, *The Scotch-Irish of Colonial Pennsylvania*, Chapel Hill, 1944, p. 185.
[3] Henry Glassie, op. cit., pp. 147 and 154.

bedroom attached, was at once kitchen, work-place, living-room and bedroom, and there is little doubt that it frequently housed some of the livestock at night. All cooking was done in the open hearth.

The log-house, like the ancestral Ulster home, was built with the clearings of the fields. Its wide open hearth was fitted with familiar gear: crane and iron pots, flesh-hook and pot-hooks, griddle and frying-pan. The crude furniture—shelves, presses and folding tables—lined the walls and left the centre of the room free.[1] An interesting variant is the double-pen log-house, consisting in its commonest form of two pens under a single roof, separated by an open passage known as the breezeway or dog trot. Originating apparently in Appalachia, it spread from the Tennessee Valley northwards into Kentucky, westwards into Missouri and Arkansas, but especially southwards into Georgia, Alabama, Mississippi and Louisiana. The dog-trot house, it has been claimed, was influenced by the through-passage of the north-west Ulster house, but its standard form owes much to Georgian fashions of symmetry and proportion. The central passage was often converted into a hall, and this style of house, translated into brick or frame, became fashionable in urban areas, for example in Tennessee. In this and other ways the log-house had a lasting effect on the traditional house-types of the Old West and beyond.

But the log-house should be seen as only one element in a complex of cultural adaptations. The Ulstermen found themselves in a land of hills and valleys, providing on the hillsides—or in the 'notches' or 'gaps'—the sites which they preferred; and although heavily forested, the 'mountain' still provided the extensive summer grazing they had been accustomed to find on the Ulster hills. It was a forest of richly varied species of trees and shrubs. The backwoodsman's principal tool, the axe, served to fell or at least to deaden the trees by girdling, but not to clear the stumps, and whereas the Germans are said to have selected level sites, grubbed up the tree roots and turned their clearings into ploughed fields, the Scotch-Irish preferred to make fresh clearings and move on once they had 'taken the good' out of the land. They were in effect practising their old 'outfield' system, adapted to a forested landscape of seemingly limitless extent. They were not tied to a plot

[1] Cf. E. E. Evans, *Irish Folk Ways*, 1957, p. 86.

of earth by a regular system of crop-rotation or any tradition of fruit-growing. The Indian methods of 'deadening' the woodlands served their purpose. A system of brush fallow—the equivalent of the Irish outfield—still characterises parts of Appalachia, and even that part of the farm which is kept under cultivation is sometimes cropped in small patches which are abandoned after two or three years. A photograph of ploughing in progress on the Virginia piedmont (Pl. 2) might have been taken in County Tyrone. Another cultural trait which characterised the backwoodsmen and which has Ulster antecedents was the practice of 'striving', the performance by rival workers of prodigious feats of strength and endurance.[1]

The Indian corn was a prolific substitute for oats and barley; and like them it was spring-sown and food for man and beast. Animal husbandry was of course an innovation, but hunting and the utilisation of the forest owed much to the Indians. The 'backwoods' life which the Scotch-Irish adopted was well named, for it took shape in the shadow of the woods and derived much of its colour, sustenance and its superstitions from them. One of the subsidiary occupations of the rural population of the Old West today, from the Carolinas to Kentucky, is root digging and herb gathering to supply the crude drug houses.[2] Growing out of the backwoodsmen's use of simples and herbal cures, the industry now utilises over a hundred plants, most of them native to the woodlands and long known to the Indians. The forest also had many species of nut- and fruit-bearing trees and supplied high quality timber in great variety—poplar, chestnut, hickory, ash, oak, dogwood and the versatile cedar—for every household use. The dogwood with its milk-white blossoms, which bring to the Old West an air of festival in May, seems to have taken the place of the Irish may tree as an ecological index, a sign of warm weather and an emblem of good luck: the tradition that corn was not planted until the dogwood flowers were fully open may well have been borrowed from the Indians.

The backwoodsmen took over not only the Indian's vast store

[1] The spirit of competition found a fertile field in North America. Its original purpose in Ireland may have been magical, but it has been interpreted as providing a stimulus towards the completion of a task, such as turf-cutting or harvesting, before the weather broke. See E. E. Evans, op. cit., p. 188.
[2] E. T. Price, 'Root Digging in the Appalachians', *The Geog. Review*, Vol. 50 (1960), pp. 1–20.

of knowledge of plants and animals and forest lore, but his passion for hunting, and with it the deerskin shirt and the stalker's moccasins.[1] Indian arrowheads provided them with gun flints.[2] They wore their hair long, Indian fashion, dressed it with bear's grease and tied it with an eel-skin or a 'whang'. Nor would Indian music, consisting of drum and flute, have been unfamiliar to Ulstermen.[3] The 'Indian fighters' took on many of the attributes of the Indian brave, and the strong silent hero of American folklore was surely born on the old frontier.

Few would agree with Arnold Toynbee that 'the impress of Red Indian savagery (on the Scotch-Irish) is the only social trace that has been left behind by these vanquished and vanished Redskins'.[4] Even this unfortunate judgement could be expressed differently, for a contemporary observer stated that the frontiersmen learnt the skills of concealment and surprise from their Indian enemies and turned them to good advantage in the struggle for political independence.[5] If in recent years the role of the Indian in the shaping of American life on the frontier has been re-evaluated,[6] less attention has been paid to his contributions in material culture. The first English accounts of the woodland Indians often pay high tribute to their cultural and agricultural standards, but very soon the colonists, and especially the puritan theologians, began to stress the barbarism, tribalism and nomadism of the Indians. These were precisely the defects which the English saw in the Irish whom they were conquering at the same period.[7] In fact, the detested nomadic habits both of the Irish and the Indians were to a considerable extent the consequence of, and a defence against, foreign invasion. But leaving this aside, the main reason for the

[1] Leather or rawhide articles of clothing would have been no novelty to the Ulster immigrants, for leather breeches were worn in some parts of the country in the eighteenth century. See G. R. Buick, *Journ. Roy. Soc. Antiquaries Ireland*, 1883–84, p. 125.
[2] Joseph Doddridge, *Notes on the Settlement and the Indian War* (1824), Pittsburgh, 1912, p. 25.
[3] Mark van Doren (ed.), *The Travels of William Bartram, 1777*, 1928, p. 206.
[4] Arnold Toynbee, op. cit., Vol. 2, p. 312.
[5] Colonel James Smith's famous account of his travels and captivity was published in Lexington, Kentucky, in 1799. Quoted in Wilcomb E. Washburn, *The Indian and the White Man*, New York, 1964, p. 265.
[6] See, for example, A. Irving Hallowell, 'The Backwash of the Frontier: The Impact of the Indian on American Culture', in Walter D. Hyman and Clifton B. Kroeber (eds.), *The Frontier in Perspective*, Madison, 1957.
[7] See D. B. Quinn, *The Elizabethans and the Irish*, Ithaca, 1966.

denigration was the need felt by the invaders to justify conquest. None was more zealous than the Ulster-Scot Presbyterian in 'smiting the enemies of the Lord'. The Indians, while accepting, for good or for ill, the material goods of white civilisation, found it so unattractive that they consciously refused to be absorbed.[1] Consequently their degraded remnants appeared to nineteenth-century historians to confirm the views of their first conquerors.

Settled agriculture had been practised in the Eastern Woodlands for millennia, and the historian's references to virgin forests are therefore as misleading as when applied to Elizabethan Ireland. Many parts of the Great Valley, for example, must have been secondary woodland, full of old clearings, and it was crossed by Indian trails. The Cherokee Indians had established a powerful 'kingdom' in the southern Appalachians,[2] and they had subsidiary hunting grounds in Shawnee territory beyond the Cumberland Mountains, their trails, which the pioneers were to follow, winding through the wind-gaps.

Other crops besides maize were taken over from the Indians: tobacco, beans of various kinds, pumpkins, squash and gourds. They all lent themselves to hand-cultivation and harvesting and demanded only the simplest of implements, spade, mattock and hoe. Like the other prolific crop of New World origin which was by this time well known in Ireland, and which the settlers took with them to North America—where it came to be known as the Irish potato—maize was cultivated by moulding or 'hilling', in the Indian fashion. It did not require a well-prepared seed-bed and its rapid growth smothered rank weeds. Moreover, the Indian methods of preparing corn for food were very similar to the Irish methods, requiring no elaborate mills or ovens. The hominy-block was a ready substitute for the knocking-stone, and hominy for porridge. Bread in cakes of many kinds (gritted bread, parched-bread, cornbread, hoecakes) was baked on the hearth—on a griddle, a bread-stick or a hoe—or in the pot-oven; and the open hearth kept its function as the focus of the home. One item listed as the pioneer housewife's helpmeet is the bundle of turkey

[1] Edmund S. Morgan, *The American Indian: Incorrigible Individualist*, Providence, 1958, p. 7.
[2] 'The Cherokee Nation' was recognised by the U.S. by treaty in 1791, although later ignored by Andrew Jackson.

feathers—a ready native replacement for the goose-wing 'tidy' of the Irish hearth.'[1]

A long list might be made of cultural needs which the Scotch-Irish immigrants and their descendants were able to satisfy, develop and exploit in their bountiful new environment. The dairyman's stave-built utensils, which in Ulster's deforested landscape had come to be made of bog-oak, could now be fashioned out of cedar and white oak in a variety of types: tubs, firkins, piggins, noggins, churns, pails and keelers. Pipe-staves were in great demand for the provision trade both at home and in Ireland, and no less than 1,170,384 staves were shipped from Philadelphia to Ireland in 1771.[2] Similarly the export of flaxseed to Ulster was a logical development.

The single-farm, we have seen, was the characteristic pioneer settlement. It is coming to be recognised that it was the Scotch-Irish who first 'filled up the mountainsides from New Hampshire to the Great Smokies' with their solitary log-houses and their corn and woodlands-pasture culture.[3] The family farm of the Old West, surrounded by its extensive woodlands 'outfield', was an Atlantic heritage, very different both from the village system of New England and from the plantation mansions of the southern tidewater. The right to claim ownership of land by possession and improvement was arrogantly assumed by colonists who had fought stubbornly for their tenant rights in Ulster; and this right was finally recognised and rationalised in the Homestead Act of 1862. Thus the single-farm became the standard settlement-type of vast areas of the American heartland.

As in Atlantic Europe the communal, commercial and religious needs of scattered farms were met by small settlement clusters at cross-roads, typically grouped around a mill, a post-office or a church. These 'unincorporated hamlets' are 'next to farms, the most ubiquitous of all settlement-types in the United States',[4] and

---

[1] For this and many detailed descriptions of pioneer life see H. S. Arnow, *Seedtime in the Cumberland*, Macmillan, 1960.

[2] Stella H. Sutherland, *Population Distribution in Colonial America* (1936), Appendix p. 322.

[3] C. M. Arensberg, 'American Communities', *The American Anthropologist* 57 (1955), nos. 1143–62, p. 155. See also C. O. Sauer in J. Leighly (ed.), *Land and Life* (1965), pp. 45–52.

[4] Glen T. Trewartha, 'The Unincorporated Hamlet', *Annals of the Ass. of Am. Geog.* 33 (1943), pp. 32–81.

they are most numerous in the region where they originated: in Pennsylvania, Maryland, Virginia, West Virginia, and Kentucky. At an early stage, before roads and towns were established, the pedlar must have played an important role in supplying scattered farms with news and trivial luxuries: he became a figure of American folklore and, since he had a flying start, founder of many a fortune in the new cities of the Middle West.

Of the many small towns established in Pennsylvania in the eighteenth century one type seems to have special associations with the Scotch-Irish. In plan it is a street-town resembling Cookstown, Beragh or Sixmilecross in County Tyrone, but with cross-streets spaced at fairly regular intervals. These towns were for the most part built by speculators in the late eighteenth century and their purpose is shown by the name Market Street often given to the main thoroughfare. They occasionally copy the name of an Ulster town, e.g. Armagh in East Wheatfield Township in Indiana County, which was laid out in 1792. In some instances, more-over, e.g. Rehrersburg, the street incorporates an elongated market place which is significantly known as 'the Diamond',[1] a word which seems to be used elsewhere in this connection only in Ulster, though it is found in some American towns outside Pennsylvania, e.g. Cleveland, Ohio. The rectangular form of the 'square' at Rehrersburg, however, is not typical of Ulster towns. Another plan represented in Pennsylvanian towns—the grid-town with central square—may also have antecedents in Ulster (e.g. Londonderry) though its roots lie in the common ground of Renaissance town-planning.[2] The central square is characteristic of numerous planned towns established in the late eighteenth century throughout the Old West. In the case of county seats the square contains the courthouse, one of the first examples[3] (later removed) being Lancaster in Lancaster County, where many Ulstermen settled. In towns established in the early nineteenth century, for example in Indiana, it was enlarged to comprise a complete block of the grid. The original purpose of the central

---

[1] I am indebted to Richard Pillsbury of West Virginia University for this information, and for sending me copies of relevant town plans. He has listed 56 examples of street-towns (with or without 'diamonds') in Pennsylvania.

[2] For example, the grid-iron town-plan which was to become the standard pattern in the New World was already known in Spanish America from about 1570.

[3] Information kindly supplied by Professor E. T. Price of the University of Oregon.

square would have been to provide parking space for market wagons, but the idea of adding a central building may well have come, like the word Diamond, from Ulster. It has been claimed that the central position of the courthouse in these towns reflects the *municipio* tradition of the American south, but the evidence seems to link it with Pennsylvania, and since it was an early feature (before 1800) of trans-Appalachian settlement and is still most frequently found in Virginia, North Carolina, Kentucky and Tennessee, there is reason to think that it was taken there by the Scotch-Irish, whose Presbyterian predilection for 'the law' was notorious.

To sum up, it is suggested that the influence of the Scotch-Irish in the making of the United States of America lay not only in their outstanding contributions to leadership in politics and education but, perhaps more significantly, in their shaping of the patterns of settlement, land-use, economy and society. They took with them the bellicose non-conformist heritage of the Atlantic ends of Europe.[1] It is a subject that calls for investigation through the interpretation of the masses of local records surviving in the Old West; but documentary evidence alone cannot fully illuminate the largely unwritten processes of cultural adaptation that are involved in pioneer settlement. What is needed is the co-operation of the social anthropologist, the cultural geographer and the student of folk-life.

[1] E. E. Evans, 'The Atlantic Ends of Europe', *The Advancement of Science*, Vol. 25 (1958), pp. 34–64.

CHAPTER V

Ulster Emigrants' Letters

by E. R. R. Green

It might be well to begin by giving some thought to what sort of people actually are emigrants and by implication to what kind of correspondence can be considered as emigrant letters. Emigration, says the *Concise Oxford Dictionary*, involves 'leaving one country to settle in another'. This means that travellers, tourists, members of the armed forces, colonial administrators and missionaries to the heathen are not emigrants nor can the letters they write be regarded as emigrant letters. The dictionary seems to take the view that expatriation and emigration are synonymous, but I think that most of us would recognise a difference. It would be seen at once, for example, in the absurdity of calling an individual an emigrant who had made a permanent home say in Paris. It follows from this that we can exclude most writers, artists and musicians who settle in some great cultural centre because they have found their home atmopshere uncongenial or lacking in necessary facilities. We may similarly exclude the fortunate few who can afford to live in the South of France or in the West Indies.

Most of those engaged in international trade, which can be taken in this case as including the production as well as the handling of certain commodities, are not emigrants either, for the reason that they are simply away on business even though it may be for years at a time. So this rules out such people as merchants and bankers in Hong Kong or Calcutta, traders in Africa or the South Seas, sugar planters in the West Indies, tea planters in Assam, or rubber planters in Malaya. Emigration must be a voluntary act, so we may also exclude those who were transported for crimes or for opposition to the government of the day or who fled to escape punishment. Yet people belonging to these otherwise dissimilar categories have this much in common, that they frequently become emigrants by making a permanent home in one of the countries of European settlement. Certainly, so far as Ireland is concerned, political refugees have in a majority of cases become emigrants. Conversely, Irish emigrants have not been averse to being regarded as exiles. What this all amounts to is that the correspondence of people living in North or South America, Australasia, or the European-settled parts of Africa should be carefully examined to see whether the writer is an emigrant or not.

There are two reasons in particular why it is necessary to be so precise in defining exactly what constitutes an emigrant. The first is that very large numbers of emigrant letters are in private hands, so it is important that people who have the good fortune to know where they are or to happen upon them should know what to look for. The second reason is indeed the main theme of this lecture; the use which the historian can make of emigrant letters. I suppose the first assumption about such a letter as a historical document would be that its importance lay in the amount of information provided about the country and particular place where the writer happened to be at the time. But in most cases the professional writer, the educated traveller, or even the temporary resident will do this far better and more accurately. Such letters then should be regarded primarily as a source of information about the emigrant rather than about the place where he settled.

The importance of the emigrant letter, in fact, is in documenting the experience of emigration. The sort of thing we can expect these letters to tell us is what the emigrant thought of his position and prospects at home and what he expected to gain by moving to a new country. They will also tell us how well the new land lived up to those expectations. We can hope to find from them how accustomed patterns of social relationships, of religious belief and practice, and of political attitudes stood up to a new environment.

Then, if we are prepared to broaden our definition somewhat to include letters sent to emigrants by those left at home or written by emigrants to each other we can hope to get a more complete impression of the emigrant experience. These emigrant letters in reverse, as they might well be called, tell a great deal about the decision to emigrate, of how people were briefed before setting out, of what fears held them back and what hopes encouraged them, and of how the cost was met and apportioned. The cross letters between emigrants explain much about their mobility in following employment opportunities and how their choice of a place to live and of a job was affected by kinship or local ties.

Now, although even a large collection of emigrant letters would not constitute a sample in the sense understood by any statistician, it may enable us to make some generalisations about emigration. The attempt to do so is admittedly something of an experiment for historians and other social scientists have made only limited use of such material. Some fifty years ago, two sociologists in the United States analysed nearly 1,000 letters which they obtained from members of the Polish immigrant community.[1] Although their interests were not in any sense historical, they nonetheless suggested a methodology which is a great deal more fruitful than simply treating emigrant letters as an accumulation of unrelated historical records.

Otherwise, I am aware of only two collections of emigrant letters which have been published. One is a volume of Norwegian letters brought out some years ago by Professor Blegen of the University of Minnesota.[2] The other is a collection of Welsh letters made by Professor Alan Conway, then at Aberystwyth.[3] The latter has the disadvantage of being almost exclusively drawn from printed sources. There is good reason to distrust emigrant letters which succeeded in being published. At the best, they have been written by people who look forward to the pleasure of seeing themselves in print. At the worst, they may be forgeries or drastically edited so as to provide propaganda either for or against emigration according to the policy of the journal. I should add that Dr Charlotte Erickson of the London School of Economics has been collecting English and Scottish emigrant letters for a number of years and hopes to publish a selection of them in the near future.

When I began collecting the letters of Irish emigrants in 1960

---

[1] W. I. Thomas and F. Znaniecki, *The Polish Peasant in Europe and America*, (5 vols., Boston, Mass., 1918–20).
[2] T. C. Blegen, *Land of their Choice* (St Paul, Minn., 1955).
[3] A. A. Conway, *The Welsh in America* (Aberystwyth, 1961).

such documents were almost non-existent in public archives.[1] My own collection has been formed by circularising libraries and archives in North America, Africa, Australia and New Zealand and by appeals in the press and on television. The response has been small but rather better on the whole than the results expected from an expensive advertising campaign. Needless to say, I have also investigated libraries and archives wherever possible. I have been fortunate enough during this time to have been fairly frequently in the United States, teaching and lecturing, and took the opportunity to visit as many archives as I could. Usually, they have yielded at least one or two letters. This fortunate result, though, generally depends on the knowledge possessed by an archivist of his own collections as 'emigrant letter' is unfortunately not a standard catalogue heading.

Special mention must be made of the success of the Public Record Office of Northern Ireland in building up a large collection of emigrant letters in a very short time. I should like to add that the National Library of Ireland in Dublin has also been most generous in copying letters and in following up leads to which I have not always been able to give immediate attention. Finally, I must express appreciation of the generous financial aid given to the project by an award from the British Association for American Studies.

The scope of the lecture series limits us to letters written from or to the United States or the thirteen colonies from which they were formed. There is an advantage in concentrating on a single country of settlement as this should sharpen the main features of the emigrant experience. Nor, it might be added, is there anything arbitrary in separating Ulster emigrants from those of Ireland as a whole. The regional economy of Ulster has, in fact, been reflected in a migration pattern distinct from that of the rest of the country.

The letters available to me are fairly evenly spread over the years from the beginning of the last century to the present day. Late seventeenth and early eighteenth-century emigrants are

[1] The Public Record Office of Northern Ireland being the outstanding exception. By 1959 it held over 380 emigrant letters. See *Deputy Keeper's Report, 1954–59* (H.M.S.O. 1966), para. 9. Reference also must be made here to the collection of over 200 letters made by Professor Arnold Schrier in 1955. These letters, although none were actually published, were used as source material for his book, *Ireland and the American Emigration, 1850–1900* (Minneapolis. Minn., 1958).

hardly represented at all. This is not very surprising; it is, after all, a long time to expect documents to survive in private hands. As we have already found, very few emigrant letters were in archives until recently. Occasional letters were printed in eighteenth-century newspapers, but they were generally propaganda either for or against the emigrant trade and their authenticity must always be in doubt. The earliest I have seen appeared in the *Pennsylvania Gazette* in October 1737 and was alleged to have been written by James Murray of New York to the Reverend Baptist Boyd of County Tyrone, Ireland.[1] The oldest manuscript letters I know are of roughly the same date; the letters written by Robert Parke to his sister Mary Valentine in County Carlow in 1725 and by William Pim to his uncles in Queen's County in 1732. Both Parke and Pim were Irish Quakers who had emigrated to Pennsylvania.[2]

The earliest Ulster letter to have turned up so far was written in 1758 by David Lindsey to his cousin Thomas Fleming in 'Pennsillvena'. A copy of this letter was received as recently as April 1965 by the Ulster-Scot Historical Society from Mr Forrest Patrick Wood of Seattle in the course of genealogical inquiries. The original was apparently discovered in a genealogy file of the Lawson family by the late Helen Bradley Lindsey of Newport, Kentucky. I should like to quote this letter at length as it is such a typical specimen for all its early date. David Lindsey shows concern for the well-being of an emigrant relative of the sort which has not changed much over the years. One of the surprising things indeed is how little the style and language of emigrant letters has altered since this was written. He begins:

> I had upertunity of reading your letter that was sent to your father-in-law, which gave me great satisfaction to hear you were all in good health and fortuned so well as to be possessed in so good a bargain of lands. We are all in good health at present. I bless God for all his mercies, and yr. uncle David is helthy and harty, and do all join in our love and compliments to you and your families and enquiring friends. I expected account oftener from you, only times being troublesome in that country with wars

[1] Earl G. Swem (ed.), *Letter of James Murray of New York to Rev. Baptist Boyd of County Tyrone, Ireland. Reprinted from the Pennsylvania Gazette, Oct. 27, 1737* (Metucken, N.J., 1925).
[2] Both letters are printed in Albert C. Myers, *Immigration of the Irish Quakers into Pennsylvania* (Swarthmore, Pa., 1902), pp. 69–71 and 373.

that we were assured that you were all dead or killed. The good
bargains of your lands in that country doe greatly encourage me
to 'pluck up my spirits and make redie for the journey, for we are
now oppressed with our lands at 8s. per acre and other improve-
ments, cutting our land in two-acre parts and quicking, and only
two years time for doing it all—yea, we cannot stand more. I
expected a letter from you more oftener, or that cusen Wm.
Fleming would come over before this time, but these things does
not discourage me to goe, only we depend on ye for directions in
the goods fitting to take to that place. I had disappointment of 20s.
worth of lining clothe I sold, and had James Hoskins' bond for the
money. The merchant ran away, and I had great truble in getting
my money, so that was deleavered. Brother John Fleming is dead,
and brother James Lindsey is married again to one Hoskins, and
his son Robert has service to his uncle, James Martin, and desires
to know if he will redeem himself if he goes over there. He is
a good favour and is willing to work for his passage till it's paid.
Your cusen in Desertmartin is all in health and joins in love to ye.
My father is very far spent, and I expect to see him buried before
I leave the place. Your father and my uncle Andrew is but tender
in health. Sarah Rickets desires to be remembered in her love to
her sister Nelly and other friends. Our living is dear in this place.[1]

And so it ends. Most emigrant letters, whatever the date, are
much like this, containing a jumble of family news of little importance to anyone any more along with occasional scraps of valuable
historical information. A good example of the latter is the evidence
for enclosure in the reference by Lindsey to 'cutting our land in
two-acre parts and quicking'. The letter shows very well the pull
of cheap land across the Atlantic and the push of the land system
at home which played so important a part in Irish emigration from
the beginning. The pressure on land would have been there in any
case as population grew, but a tenant system of land holding
inevitably aroused animosity against those who controlled the
supply of the scarce commodity. There is a reference in the letter
to redemptioners or indentured servants, as they were also called,
which needs some explanation. Robert Lindsey was proposing to
make use of a common system whereby those who had no funds
to meet the cost of the passage to America undertook to work
without wages for a number of years.

Finally, I think this early specimen is excellent proof of the

[1] Public Record Office of Northern Ireland, T. 2539.

92

importance of reverse letters, as I suggested we might call those written from Ulster to the emigrants, and of the necessity of treating them in effect as emigrant letters.

The broader significance of emigrant letters can only be appreciated on a comparative basis, so I now propose to deal with them in this way. No part of the emigrant experience is better documented than the original setting out from home to a far country. The reasons are obvious. For one thing, most people will write at least one long letter on leaving home no matter how badly they may turn out as correspondents later on. Again, the first experience of travelling away from familiar surroundings will produce a livelier interest and result in sharper observation than on subsequent journeyings. The chances of survival of the first letter sent on leaving home are, of course, good. The sentimental value of such a letter must always be high, but even more so in the days when the separation was likely to be final.

The general impression is that conditions of emigrant travel were harsh in the extreme, at least in the days of sail. This is not borne out by the accounts in most emigrant letters. Certainly, in most of those written by young, unmarried emigrants the Atlantic crossing is described pretty well in terms of a holiday. Living conditions on the ships were cramped, but so were those in farmhouses at home. The initial terror of rough seas soon passed over. The diet on the voyage was not unfamiliar as the emigrants brought their own food with them; oatmeal, potatoes, bacon and a supply of sugar and tea or coffee bought for the voyage. Generally speaking, deaths on shipboard were confined to children, often from measles, or to old people. Still, this favourable picture no doubt must be balanced by undocumented losses through shipwreck or impressment in time of war, the unfortunate individuals concerned perhaps perishing without ever having time to write to their people at home. Sometimes an emigrant survived to tell the tale of a particularly hazardous voyage. Such a one was John O'Raw who spent five months in getting from Belfast to South Carolina in 1806. His ship sailed in late November and after experiencing six weeks of continuous storm ran aground on the island of Bermuda in fair weather and was lost. The captain refused to take any further responsibility for his passengers who were forced to charter a sloop to carry them to Charleston in which they again almost perished in a storm. As it was, O'Raw had been fortunate not to be pressed into the Royal Navy while in Bermuda like some of the young men among the passengers.[1]

Interestingly enough, the mobility characteristic of Americans is evident with emigrants from an early date. Hester Habersham, for example, in letters to her sister, Helen Lawrence, at Coleraine, in the 1770s seems to regard the long voyage from Savannah, Georgia, to England or Ireland without undue excitement.[2] Indeed, it seems that so long as people had the funds to go back and forth across the Atlantic they did not take a much more serious view of the difficulties and perils than we do today.

When they reached America, emigrants were free to take up a wide variety of work. Again, it is necessary to remind ourselves of the imperfect nature of emigrant letters as a sample. The unskilled are obviously badly under-represented as are the failures. In the eighteenth century the aim of most emigrants no doubt was to take up farming where land was cheap and abundant and free of rent and tithe. Unfortunately, the number of letters which have survived from this time is too small to hazard any generalisation.

After 1800, when far more emigrant letters are available for study, the characteristic emigrant seems to be a young man of around twenty years of age with a good family background of industrious and prudent small or medium farmer stock, who has been given a fair education, and who already has some idea of where to go and what to do in the United States. Even more important, he has a sizeable number of contacts in America who he believes, usually with justification, will be prepared to help him. These contacts were almost invariably limited to family and neighbourhood connections and depended on large-scale migration for effectiveness. As is well known, the tide of emigration ran more strongly from Ireland after 1815 than ever before, caused in the main by the post-war fall from a high level of farming prosperity.

Most young emigrants of what might be called this middle-class type had no intention of taking up manual labour if they could avoid it. The ideal for them was to secure employment with a merchant or shopkeeper. John Phillips of Lisburn, writing from upstate South Carolina in March 1819, says that 'a man who can set up a small store in the country is superior to any other. He will

---

[1] John O'Raw, Charleston, S. C., to his parents, 1 April 1809. Communicated by Mrs Michael Tierney, Dublin.
[2] Hester Habersham, Savannah, Ga., to Helen Lawrence, n.d. P.R.O.N.I., D. 955/12.

sell nothing but what he will have 30 per cent or more.' Phillips himself initially agreed in Charleston to take a school-teaching job in the back country at $300 a year. When he was disappointed in this, he turned to carpentering and in partnership with a relative speculated in the building of a Methodist church.[1]

Employment as a clerk in a frontier store marked the beginning of a successful business career for many a young Ulster emigrant. Such a position provided the opportunity either of being admitted to a partnership or of amassing sufficient capital to go into business on one's own. Although the movements of the business cycle in the United States in the early nineteenth century were sharp and sudden and caused heavy mortality in business enterprises, it was in consequence all the easier for new businesses to start up. Also, the possibilities of expansion in new frontier communities were much greater than in an Irish country town. An apt illustration of this point would be John T. Pirie and Samuel Carson, two of the founders of the great Chicago department store of Carson, Pirie, Scott, whose original intention was to set up in the drapery business in Cookstown, County Tyrone.[2]

Somewhat of a second-best in the eyes of the young emigrant was school-teaching. No doubt there was an acute shortage of teachers in the States in consequence both of the unattractiveness of an occupation with a more or less fixed income level and also of the very large numbers of children in a young and rapidly growing population. In any case, emigrant letters abound in references to friends and relatives running schools of their own or employed as teachers.

The evidence of emigrant letters suggests that Ulster emigrants at any rate were still anxious to establish themselves on the land until well on in the nineteenth century when it is generally assumed that emigration was mainly directed towards towns. A tradesman like John Ard of Ballynahinch worked in a machine shop at Westfield in Chatauqua County, New York, but also had a small-holding on which he could keep a cow and raise much of what he ate. This was in 1871, and it had taken him most of his working life to manage that much.[3] Andrew Greenlees of Magheramorne

---

[1] John Phillips, Fairfield, S.C., to James Phillips, Lisburn, Co. Antrim, 1819. P.R.O.N.I., T. 1449.
[2] *National Cyclopedia of American Biography*, Vol. VIII, pp. 53–4.
[3] John Ard, Westfield, N.Y., to ——, 1871. P.R.O.N.I., T. 1597.

emigrated to New York about 1850 and set about learning to be an ironmoulder. As he said, 'A young man can do better to take a trade than to be knocked about by the farmer'. Greenlees had himself become a farmer by 1857, but it would seem that he had insufficient capital and was unable to keep his head above water. In 1874 he became a homesteader in Kansas, his letters from there giving a vivid picture of the back-breaking business of building a house and offices and of creating a farm out of the wilderness.[1]

The unskilled man was helped by his mobility in a country where he had no ties of family or birthplace, especially if he was still unmarried. Edward McNally was probably a characteristic example. Unable to find work in Philadelphia when he landed, he set out for Pittsburgh but ran out of money before he got there, so he took a job on the railroad. When he had finally saved up enough to get to Pittsburgh, he found there was a cholera epidemic there, and thought it wise to go on to Cincinnati. Once more, he found himself penniless and had to fall back again on railroad employment. As soon as summer came he went to work with a farmer and then in winter took a job as a flatboatman, handling shipments of fireclay and firebrick. That did not last either, and he again worked on the railroad. At the time of writing the letter which chronicled all these wanderings he had at last succeeded in finding a job in a machine shop which paid the equivalent of a guinea a week in wages.[2]

Discussion of the kind of work the emigrant did leads naturally to his reaction to America. Again, it is well to remember the imperfect nature of the sample; the unsuccessful are less likely to write than those who have something worth telling. Even when this is taken into account, the favourable reaction of the emigrants to American conditions is impressive. They were particularly struck with the dignity of labour in America. James Richey emigrated from near Lisburn to Philadelphia in 1818 and after an anxious interval secured employment with a storekeeper in western Kentucky. In writing home he described his encounter with his prospective employer as follows:

[1] Andrew Greenlees, Plattsburg, N.Y., to his brother, 1 Nov. 1852. P.R.O.N.I., T. 2046/1.
[2] Edward McNally, Middletown, N.Y., to Capt. William McNally, Portaferry, Co. Down, 1851. P.R.O.N.I., T. 1448.

I went up to him with my hat in my hand as humble as any Irishman and asked him if he wanted a person of my description (put on yr hat said he, we are all a free people here we all enjoy equal freedom & privilages)—he hesitated a little and said I believe I do. He asked me where I was from and how long since I landed & some other questions and we closed our bargain.[1]

Andrew Greenlees, to quote him again, wrote in 1853 that 'this is a free country, Jack's as good as his master, if he don't like one then go to another. Plenty of work and plenty of wages, plenty to eat and no landlords, that's enough, what more does a man want.'[2]

When an emigrant wrote home of high American wages and good working conditions, it might reasonably be supposed that he would encourage relatives and neighbours to join him. Yet in the main emigrants were as cautious about advising others to come to America as they were unrestrained in their praise of the country. The following comment from a County Down emigrant in 1785 is typical:

I have not been at a loss for work nor lost no time since I came to America. As for encouraging any person to come here, I will not, but if any friends or acquaintances comes, I would be glad to see them.[3]

Paradoxical though such an attitude may seem it was prudent in the circumstances. The immigrant group had many of the characteristics of an extended family and its members were under similar obligations to a new arrival as would have been expected by a relative at home. This caution though is a different matter from the sense of alienation which sometimes appears when the emigrant writes of America, especially in the letters of those who have grown old in the new country. It is well expressed in a letter from a Tyrone man in New York, written not so many years ago.

But Michael, never think of leaving it to come to this man's country. It takes one half a lifetime to become accustomed to the

[1] James Richey, Trenton, Ky., to his parents, Moyrusk, Co. Antrim, 13 Aug. 1819. Collection of the author.
[2] Greenlees, Plattsburg, N.Y., to his brother, 27 May 1853. P.R.O.N.I., T. 2046/4.
[3] Andrew Martin, Morland Township, Philadelphia County, Pa., to his father, 10 Aug. 1785. P.R.O.N.I., T. 1752/2.

U.S. and by that time one is grown so old that the enjoyment is gone out of life.[1]

Emigrants could not avoid responsibility so easily where members of their own families were concerned. Indeed, one of the most important continuing family obligations of the emigrant was to facilitate subsequent departures for the New World. He decided when brothers and sisters should emigrate, he often paid for their passages on the tacit understanding that a loan was being made, and they lived with him on arrival until they could be placed in employment. It would be tedious to quote examples of these arrangements which are a constant theme of emigrant correspondence in any case. Usually the emigrant is to be found urging patience. It was important for his own standing in a new community that subsequent arrivals did reasonably well and proved a credit to him. This in turn depended on his ability to find them satisfactory employment. So he was not too anxious to be followed by members of his family until he had established himself. Married brothers and sisters he was not particularly anxious to see in any case. A family has housing troubles, is less mobile, and costly to maintain while its head looks for a job. The family of a failure or of a widow could also prove a costly burden.

The number of letters incidentally in which there is an almost contemporary insistence on the importance of a good education is impressive. This cannot have been because of any serious gap between Irish and American levels of education, at any rate in the nineteenth century. It was based rather on a shrewd recognition of the need for better than average qualifications if a good start were to be made in a strange country. Hugh McCloskey, who became a prominent citizen of New Orleans, in writing home in 1866 advises a nephew and namesake to wait for another two years before emigrating. 'Let your father', he writes, 'send you to a good school and I will pay the expenses' for 'I do not wish to see you here without something like a fair English education.'[2]

As well as assistance in paying fares and in finding work for subsequent emigrants, direct financial help was often expected at home. A characteristic example of the strong sense of family duty

[1] Peter McCullagh, Mineola, N.Y., to Michael Murphy, 14 May 1852. Communicated by the Irish Folklore Commission, Dublin.
[2] Hugh McCloskey, New Orleans, to his nephew, Coleraine, Co. Londonderry, 22 July 1866. P.R.O.N.I., T. 1767.

among emigrants appears in this letter from San Francisco, written
by a Tyrone man in 1895 in which he says 'dear father, if ever you
want any money let me know, if I have only one shilling and you
want you get the half of it'. He sent a present of £2 and asked his
father to buy some snuff with the money and also 'a good strong
pound of tea' for his mother. This man was employed by a coal
dealer at the time and the height of his ambition was to work on
the street cars, 'a nice clean job'.[1]

The correspondence of individuals who voluntarily shouldered
such a heavy burden of family responsibility is bound to be an
important source of information about the family itself. While it
would be a mistake to pursue this subject any further when our
concern with family relationships is limited to their connection
with emigration, it is worth making a reference in passing to the
importance of emigrant letters as original material for the study
of the family. It should be remembered, too, that these letters are
often unique documents in the sense of having been written by
people of an educational and social level otherwise unlikely to
commit their ideas to paper.

It is remarkable how very large a proportion are in fact family
letters. Indeed, a reading of them gives the impression that social
relations in Ulster were virtually confined to the family group.
While it is possible that correspondence with people who were
not relatives was liable to a higher mortality, the fact remains that
in most emigrant letters inquiries about people who were not
connected with the family are very limited in number.

As source material for family relationships emigrant letters are
admittedly deficient as those whose reason for emigration was
family conflict are unrepresented, and they were no doubt a
sizeable proportion of the total. Still, they are not wholly undocumented for there are frequent references in letters to those
who failed to correspond whether because of bad blood or simple
carelessness.

After personal news and family matters, religion is probably the
subject most frequently met with in emigrant letters. Indeed, one
might well say that this was personal news of a most important
kind. Most Ulster emigrants had and still have a strong religious
background and knew that their relatives were concerned about

[1] P. Brown, San Francisco, to his father, Carnycoughan, Co. Tyrone, 4 Dec. 1895.
Collection of the author.

both their spiritual and material well-being. There are noticeable differences in attitude from one age to the next as might be expected. In the nineteenth century there was a stronger sense of a Divine Providence ordering all things and a readier acceptance of misfortune and disaster. There were also differences of custom which made it necessary to describe death-bed scenes, for example in what would now be regarded as harrowing detail, but in the belief, no doubt justified in those days, that relatives would be comforted. For Protestant emigrants, the presence of familiar church organisations greatly helped assimilation and was also an assurance to those at home.

Now that the matter has been raised, mention must be made of the importance of emigrant letters in documenting the process of assimilation into American society. This is a fascinating subject, but it is necessary to remember that it is also a very large one. We could easily become sidetracked into a lengthy discussion of the nature of the American society in which the immigrant had to find a place and of the character of the American patriotism with which he must come to terms. Certainly, for his peace of mind it was necessary for the immigrant to build a bridge between his old and his new identity. Gratitude for the opportunity of American life is in most instances the key to the immigrant's new loyalty. America was the best country because it offered the most. In America, too, one could gain acceptance by working hard and being successful. This attitude is very clearly expressed, even in the early days of the Republic, in a letter written in 1789 by John Dunlap, himself a distinguished immigrant, to his brother-in-law in Strabane in which he says:

> The young men of Ireland who wish to be free and happy should leave it and come here as quick as possible. There is no place in the world where a man meets so rich a reward for good conduct and industry as in America.[1]

On a cruder level assimilation could involve rejection of Ireland as a place of poverty and frustration. There is a good example of this in a letter written home to County Londonderry by John Sinclair from California in 1883:

[1] John Dunlap, Philadelphia, Pa., to Robert Rutherford, Strabane, 12 May 1789. P.R.O.N.I., T. 1336/1/22.

> You need not wright to me about going back. I will not go back.
> That country wood not do with me now. I stead to long in it. If
> I had left 15 years ago it would be all right. From the first day I
> landed in California my pocket never wanted money. When I was
> in Ireland I could not say that anny day.[1]

These are only two quotations, and it might almost be said that
each immigrant made his own adjustment to America which could
also alter a good deal as the years went by, so that it would be
unwise to rush into generalisations about this part of the emigrant
experience.

Finally, after having talked throughout in terms of social
analysis, a word must be said about the very real value which these
letters can have as historical sources. A Quaker emigrant, for
example, in writing to Thomas Greer of Dungannon in June 1771,
gives a valuable account of the Regulator rising in North Carolina
which had been crushed by the battle of the Alamance the previous
month. He tells in his letter how the leader of the Regulators,
Herman Husband, was brought up among Quakers but later
'denied . . . for his captious snarling'.[2] A letter written by James
Sloan from Nauvoo in 1842 to his cousins in Detroit provides
interesting information about the Mormons. It seems that Sloan
had once been a solicitor in Dungannon, and by his own account
had now become a person of prominence among the Latter-Day
Saints.[3]

A quite remarkable example is the long first-hand account of
the bombardment of Fort Sumter contained in two letters written
by Private John Thompson of the 1st U.S. Artillery to his father
in County Londonderry and which deserves to be quoted at some
length:

> As the smoke began to clear away a little and our batteries about to
> be opened more generally some excitement caused our cannoneers

[1] John S. Sinclair, Healdsburg, Calif., to Margaret Graham, Draperstown, Co.
Londonderry, 1883. P.R.O.N.I., D. 1497/1/2.
[2] John McDonnell, Wilmington, N.C., to Thomas Greer, Dungannon, 2 June 1771.
P.R.O.N.I., D. 1044/294.
[3] James Sloan, Nauvoo, Ill., to Andrew McReynolds, Detroit, 27 Mar. 1842. The
original of this letter is in the Illinois State Historical Society Library. A copy is
available at P.R.O.N.I., T. 2304. Portions have been published in the *Journal of the
Illinois State Historical Society Quarterly*, 1953. I am indebted to Dr P. A. M. Taylor for
the information that there is a note on Sloan's career in Juanita Brooks (Ed.), On
The Mormon Frontier (Salt Lake City, 1964), Vol. I p. 15, n. 33.

to congregate on the left where I was stationed. All were armed with their muskets. It turned out to be Col. Wigfall with a white flag. Myself and another countryman were at the embrasure when the individual above mentioned made his appearance, and we stubbornly refused him admittance for a while, but he begged so hard, exhibited the flag he carried and even surrendered his sword, that at last we helped him in. He begged us to stop firing. An officer answered 'We obey no orders here but those of Major Anderson'. He then desired to be shown to the Major who at this moment made his appearance. He begged the Major 'For God's sake to stop firing and they would grant any terms'. This the Major after a little deliberation deemed satisfactory and the word was passed 'cease firing'. Previous to this however Wigfall had been waving his handkerchief from an embrasure, but the smoke was so thick that it could not be seen, and the batteries who were not aware of Wigfall's presence still kept firing. At the rebel gentleman's request the white flag was shown from our ramparts, and the firing ceased. As soon as all was quiet the flag of truce was hauled down, and our Commander submitted or rather dictated his terms; which were that we should leave with the honors of war, salute our flag, and be furnished with transportation anywhere North we desired. Thus ended the fight and here I am without a scratch, no one being wounded in the fight but the man above aluded to. I forgot to mention that during the fire on the second day our flag was shot down, but it only remained down a few moments when it again floated from our ramparts nailed with tenpenny nails to a new stick.[1]

It should hardly be necessary to point out that emigrant letters are a rich source for the economic history of the United States. They document the activities of all kinds of people, whether merchants, planters, professional men, storekeepers, farmers, or wage earners. They describe conditions in all kinds of industries and in different sections of the country. They are even a useful source of statistical information, for emigrants were fond of sending home lists of American wages and prices, knowing that they would be of interest.

This is all I have to say of the value of emigrant letters as a historical source. Much of it, no doubt, applies equally to other

[1] John Thompson, Fort Sumter, South Carolina, to his father, Articlave, Co. Londonderry, 14 Feb. 1861, and same to same, Fort Hamilton, N.Y., 28 April 1861. P.R.O.N.I., T. 1585. These letters have been published, Brian Hutton, 'Two Letters from Fort Sumter', *Irish Sword*, Vol. V (1961–2), pp. 179–83.

countries and regions, and it is to be hoped that greater use will be made of such material by historians of emigration in the future. As I said earlier on, the letters are important primarily in documenting the emigrant experience. They could, therefore, be described as documents of social history, although I must admit that I am no great believer in drawing distinctions between different kinds of history. Clearly, the letters do possess a wider significance as historical documents *per se* in many cases, although a critical historian must be conscious of the highly subjective nature of the material and of the limited knowledge and experience of many of the writers. Surprisingly, perhaps, many of the letters can be read with enjoyment, for Ulster emigrants often wrote well. I had hardly expected as much when I began collecting, and this has been an unlooked-for reward of the labour of research.

Index

Index

Index

Index

Index

Witherspoon, Rev. John,—*cont.*
  service, 29; leadership and personality, 28; philosophy, 29
Wood, Forrest Patrick, 91
Woodmason, 19
Woodrow family, 2
Woodrow, Janet, mother of Woodrow Wilson, 3

Woodrow, Thomas, grandfather of Woodrow Wilson, 2, 4
World Student Movement, 16
Wren, Sir Christopher, 34

Yale University, 30
Y.M.C.A., 16